STUDIES OF ENGLISH MYSTICS

STUDIES OF ENGLISH MYSTICS

ST MARGARET'S LECTURES
1905

BY WILLIAM RALPH INGE, M.A., D.D.

> "Noli foras ire, in te redi.   In interiore homine
> habitat veritas ; et si animam mutabilem inveneris,
> transcende te ipsum."
>
> —AUGUSTINE, *De Vera Religione*, 72.

Essay Index Reprint Series

BOOKS FOR LIBRARIES PRESS
FREEPORT, NEW YORK

First Published 1906
Reprinted 1969

LIBRARY OF CONGRESS CATALOG CARD NUMBER:
69-17578

PRINTED IN THE UNITED STATES OF AMERICA

PREFACE

THESE Lectures were delivered in the Church of St Margaret's, Westminster, on Wednesday afternoons during Lent, 1905. They cover part of the same ground as my Bampton Lectures of 1899; but the selected writers are discussed more fully, and the Introductory Lecture embodies the results of further study since the Oxford course was written. Of the books referred to, two, *The Ancren Riwle* and *The Scale of Perfection*, are not very easy to procure at present. The former is one of the Camden Society's publications, and the latter, I understand, is soon to be edited again, the older editions being out of print. There is an excellent edition of Julian of Norwich, by Miss Warrack; and parts of

William Law have recently been reprinted.
Canon Overton's *Life of William Law* should
also be read by those who are interested in
the author of *A Serious Call* and *The Spirit
of Prayer.*

W. R. INGE.

CONTENTS.

LECTURE I

ON THE PSYCHOLOGY OF MYSTICISM

GOD has spoken by the prophets at sundry times and in divers manners. He fulfils Himself in many ways, lest one good custom should corrupt the world. Revelation — the *unveiling* of the Divine to human apprehension —should not be regarded as a particular mode of communicating Divine truth, differing from other modes by its immediacy or externality. The antithesis between natural and revealed is misleading, for the religion of nature, so far as it is true, is one kind of revealed religion. The antithesis of "natural" is not "revealed," but non-natural or supernatural; the classification implies an exclusive claim on behalf of certain facts to be unique and incommensurable with other facts. But in the truest sense, all religion is natural, and all religion is revealed.

A

Our nature is what God intended us to grow
into ; and since, in the beautiful words of
Augustine, He "made us for Himself, our
hearts are unquiet until they rest in Him."
But if we thus claim for our nature its royal
rights, if we say that our nature is to be like
God, to attain the stature of the fulness of
Christ ; if we assert that the whole law may be
briefly comprehended in the old sayings "know
thyself" and "be thyself," we are at once
confronted with the paradox that the self-
centred life is spiritual death. As individuals
we are not self-sufficing, we are not independent. Our minds are no pure mirrors
in which the beauty and wisdom of the
Divine mind may shine reflected. We cannot,
for the most part, find God unaided. He
has spoken to the prophets, not to us. This
is why we have needed, and still need, the
word revelation. Revelation is the unveiling
of some Divine truth which we could not
have discovered for ourselves, but which,
when it is shown to us by others to whom
God has spoken, we can recognise as Divine.
There can be no revelation which is purely

external; such a communication would be
partly unnoticed, and partly misunderstood.
There must be the answering witness of the
Spirit within us that this is the voice of
God; but the voice comes to us first from
without, through the mouth of those whom
God has honoured by making them His
spokesmen. A "mystery," in the New
Testament, is always something which has
been revealed, but in this manner.

It is therefore necessary for us, who are
neither saints nor prophets, to sit at the feet
of those who have seen the mysteries of the
Kingdom of God. It may be that we shall
never share their higher experiences. Strictly
speaking, visions of Divine truth are not
communicable. What can be described and
handed on is not the vision itself, but the
inadequate symbols in which the seer tries
to represent what he has experienced, to preserve it in his memory, and to impart it to
others. But such experiences, which rather
possess a man than are possessed by him, are
in their nature as transient as the glories of
a sunset. Memory preserves only a pale

reflection of them, and language, which was
not made for such purposes, fails lamentably
to reproduce even that pale reflection. Those
only can understand the mind of the prophet
or saint who can supply what is lacking in
his words from their own hearts, renewing
from the fire within them the lustre and the
glow which his descriptions strive ineffectually
to render permanent. But, nevertheless, the
fact that such experiences have been enjoyed
by many, who have expressed their unshaken
conviction that God has thus spoken to them,
is of the greatest value to us. These revelations may guide and encourage and comfort
us throughout our lives. They may give us
confidence to believe in some dim whispers
which have come to ourselves, and which
otherwise we might hardly dare to trust.
Moreover, their lives and their counsels may
show us under what conditions such revelations are possible. They may tell us where
to look, how to look, and what to look for.
The lives of the saints are thus a very
important part of religious literature. Hagiology has fallen into discredit because in

time past it was written for edification, and
not for truth. Any story that the biographer
thought honourable to the saint, and conducive
to faith and devotion, was inserted without
investigation. What Newman called the
"illative" faculty was allowed to run riot.
We desire no more religious romances of
the old sort. The strict truth is good enough
for us. If we can arrive at it, we shall find
a reinforcement to Christian faith of enormous
value. For Christianity is a very concrete
practical thing. It is, as John Smith, the
Cambridge Platonist, said, a Divine life, not
a Divine science. It is embodied in great
personalities more adequately than in any
philosophical systems or doctrinal formulas.
It found its complete expression in the Person
of the Incarnate Christ ; and, after the Gospels,
it is in the lives of His best disciples that we
shall find its brightest illustrations. Those
who have the privilege of knowing a living
saint in the flesh have the best opportunities
of all, of understanding what Christianity is.
The great saints of the past can only be
known by their books, or by the books of

others about them; and those books will be most valuable which more fully and clearly reveal the personality of their authors.

Since the vision of God is the culminating point, not of any one faculty, even of the moral conscience, but of our whole nature, transfigured into the likeness of Him whom, unless we are like Him, we cannot see as He is; and since the diverse faculties, which in their several ways bear witness to God, are developed in very different proportions by different individuals, we should expect to find that there are many paths up God's holy hill, though all meet at the top. The conditions laid down in Psalm xv. are no doubt inexorable. Only he who has clean hands and a pure heart, who is humble and sincere, charitable and upright, can ascend into the hill of the Lord, or rise up in His holy place. But the intuition of eternal truth is no monopoly of the contemplative recluse, or of the philosopher, or of the poet, or of the man of action. The perfect Christian would cultivate and consecrate heart, intellect, imagination, practical energy, in an harmonious manner, and would be brought near to God by all parts of his nature acting together. But *non omnia possumus omnes.* God gave some apostles, some prophets, some evangelists, some pastors and teachers. All these worketh one and the self-same Spirit, dividing to every man severally as He will.

The life of devotion has its mystical state, when the God whom the saint has striven to love with all his heart and mind and soul and strength, for whom he has renounced all dear domestic ties, all ambition, and all pleasure, reveals Himself in mysterious intercourse to the inner consciousness, in a vision, perhaps, of the suffering Redeemer, or as an unseen presence speaking words of love and comfort.

The intellectual life has its mystical state, when the religious philosopher, whose thoughts have long been concentrated upon the deeper problems of existence, endeavouring to find the unity which underlies all diversity, the harmony which reconciles all contradictions, seems to behold what he sought in a blank trance which imposes silence on all the faculties, even the restless discursive intellect, and unites the thinker for a few moments with the primal source of all thought, the ineffable One. Such was the goal of the "intellect in love" (νοῦς ἐρῶν) of Plotinus, and the *amor intellectualis Dei* of Spinoza.

The poet's worship of nature has its mystical state, when in Platonic fashion the admiration of beautiful forms, either human or in God's other handiwork, has led him up to a vision of Divine beauty. As Spenser sings :—

"The meanes, therefore, which unto us is lent
Him to behold is on his workes to looke,
Which he hath made in beauty excellent,
And in the same, as in a brasen booke,
To reade enregistred in every nooke
His goodnesse, which his beautie doth declare ;
For all that's good is beautifull and faire.
Thence gathering plumes of perfect speculation,
To impe the wings of thy high flying mynd,
Mount up aloft through heavenly contemplation,
From this darke world, whose damps the soule do blynd,
And, like the native brood of eagles kynd,
On that bright Sunne of glorie fix thine eyes,
Clear'd from grosse mists of fraile infirmities."

The scientific worship of nature has its mystical state. Science is a patient conversion of insight into sight, and the investigator is lighted throughout his labours by the torch of the imagination, without which natural phenomena are disconnected, dull, and spiritless. The scientific imagination creates a religion—not the old religion of nature, which peopled the woods with Dryads, and saw "old Proteus rising from the sea," but a pure, humble, disinterested reverence and worship for the vastness and splendour and majesty of the universe. This worship may daunt and oppress the spirit, as in Tennyson's fine poem called *Vastness* :—

"Spring and summer and autumn and winter, and all these old revolutions of earth,
All new-old revolutions of empire—change of the tide, what is all of it worth?
What is it all if we all of us end but in being our own corpse-coffins at last,
Swallow'd in vastness, lost in silence, drown'd in the depths of a meaningless past?"

Or it may awaken a sense of sublimity and magnificence such as the cramped universe of pre-scientific thought and imagination could hardly inspire. Such is the inspiration of Victor Hugo's tremendous poem, *L'Abîme*, in which the cosmical feeling for nature receives perhaps its grandest expression.

B

First, the spirit of Man boasts of his conquests :—

" Le monde à ma voix tremble et change . . .
Rien sans moi.   La nature ébauche ; je termine.
Terre, je suis ton roi."

Then the Earth-spirit mocks his pride :—

"Tu t'en vas dans la cendre, et moi je reste au jour ;
J'ai toujours le printemps, l'aube, les fleurs, l'amour ;
Je suis plus jeune après des millions d'années."

But Saturn reduces the earth to insignificance, and the Sun Saturn.   The glorious stars Sirius, Aldebaran, and Arcturus despise the sun, with its dim light and paltry cluster of attendant planets ; the bird-like comet, terror of the night, speeds past the stars like so many grains of mustard seed ; the Zodiac, the Milky Way, the spectral "worlds not realised" of Nebulæ that whiten the darkness, a boundless ocean of dream-worlds, utter their vaunts as they pass before the poet's eye : till the Infinite speaks one line :—

" L'être multiple vît dans mon unité sombre,"

and God says :—

" Je n'aurais que souffler, et tout serait de l'ombre."

The immanent pantheism, or "monism" as its votaries prefer to call it, which is the creed of most scientists who are religious, is a real religion, which only ignorance and prejudice can stigmatise as "infidelity." In so far as it culminates in an immediate *feeling* of being enveloped by the all-embracing Spirit of the cosmos, or, in Huxley's words, "in the sense of growing oneness with the great Spirit of abstract truth," it is a mystical religion.

The sympathetic study of human character, in much the same spirit in which Wordsworth studied nature, may lead to a kind of mysticism of a distinctive type, as we shall see in a later lecture devoted to Robert Browning.

The active life also may issue in a thoroughly mystical faith, as may be seen in the lives of soldier - mystics like Colonel Gardiner, who was slain at Prestonpans in 1745, and Charles Gordon, the knight without fear and without reproach, who fell at Khartoum. Men of this type see the hand of God everywhere. Life for them is as sacramental, as full of "mysteries" in the Greek sense of the word, as to the Platonic philo-

sopher or the poet of nature. But there
is a very striking difference in the kind of
sacramental symbolism which these two classes
of mystics seek and find in the external world.
The active, practical worker demands a
spiritual world-order in which spiritual facts
happen in time, just as his own spiritual
activities are devoted to making things happen
in time. The philosopher and the poet do
not want to make anything happen, but to
discover and understand and set a value upon
what always happens. Hence their religious
symbols are quite different. The active man
craves for evidences of Divine intervention
—for supernaturalism in some form; the
philosopher and poet make no such demand,
and the religious man of science regards belief
in miracle as a kind of blasphemy. Amiel
says that "miracle is a vision of the Divine
behind nature." Yes; but of the Divine
energising and altering the face of nature,
even as the active man would fain leave his
mark on the world, as an unique force acting
upon it. This is no place for a discussion
upon miracles, a subject which lies quite out-

side the scope of these lectures; but for those who are interested in current controversies I would suggest that much light is thrown upon the attitude of the two parties by the considerations which I have just suggested. The man who wishes to understand the world will have different religious symbols from him who wishes to leave his mark upon it.

Does this enumeration exhaust the varieties of mystical religion? I think not. A recent writer on the psychology of religion gives us the following definition. "Mysticism is that attitude of mind which divines and moves toward the spiritual in the common things of life, not a partial and occasional operation of the mind under the guidance of far-fetched analogies."[1] The last clause is directed against that bastard type of mysticism which flourishes luxuriantly among the Neo-Catholic *littérateurs* in France, and which is illustrated by the later novels of Huysmans. The definition is a good one, and is valuable as claiming for the trivial round, the common

---

[1] Granger, *The Soul of a Christian*, p. 41.

task, the power to waft us upward to the very footstool of God's throne. It is most important that we should recognise the sacramental value of mere right action, even of the most commonplace kind. Not, of course, that the action itself has this value; it is valuable because it is the expression of our habitual view of things and events and men and ourselves. Our habitual point of view is fatally incomplete unless it finds expression in habitual action. "The intellect by itself moves nothing," as Aristotle said. Beautiful thoughts hardly bring us any nearer to God until they are acted upon. "No one," says Martineau, "can have a true idea of right, until he does it; any genuine reverence for it, till he does it often, and with cost; any peace ineffable in it, till he does it always and with alacrity." The religion of right conduct is no doubt frequently contrasted with the mystical type. The religious man who begins and ends with obedience to his conscience, and devotion to duty, is not a mystic. There are many noble characters who have little or no affinity to mystical religion. Such

persons will echo the words of Christina
Rossetti :—

> " We are of those who tremble at thy Word,
>   Who faltering walk in darkness towards our close
>   Of mortal life, by terrors curbed and spurred,—
>   We are of those.
>   Not ours the heart thy loftiest love hath stirred,
>   Not such as we thy lily and thy rose,
>   Yet, Hope of those who hope with hope deferred,
>   We are of those."

Nevertheless it is the fact that the habitual
performance of the humblest daily duties has
often developed the highest spirituality of
character, with a vivid consciousness of the
presence of God within and around us, a
profound conviction that communion with
Him takes place by prayer, and an intuitive
certainty of Divine truth which is essentially
mystical.

We have seen that this intuitive certainty
or conviction, this sense of immediate contact
with the supersensual world, is common to
many classes of minds. The next question
will naturally be, what authority do these
intuitions carry with them? There are some
who think that the whole assumption of an

inner light, granted to favoured persons, is a mischievous delusion, and that the only safe guides to Divine truth are external revelation and common-sense. Such would seem to be the opinion which underlies John Stuart Mill's definition of mysticism, as being "neither more nor less than ascribing objective existence to the subjective creations of our own faculties, to ideas and feelings of the mind; and believing that by watching and contemplating those ideas of its own making, it can read in them what takes place in the world without." Even Mill, however, in his dry way, cannot help appreciating the economic value, so to speak, of an inexhaustible fund of inward happiness which enriches A without impoverishing B; and accordingly he recommends the study of Wordsworth's poems. "From them," he says, "I seemed to learn what would be the perennial sources of happiness, when all the greater evils of life shall have been removed. And I felt myself at once better and happier as I came under their influence." This experience should have taught Mill that we cannot trust common-sense to draw the line sharply and infallibly between dreams and realities, when the higher spiritual truths are in question. No doubt, as Leslie Stephen says, "all mixture of dreams and realities involves distortion of facts." But what he calls dreams are not necessarily phantoms of the imagination. They may be symbols inadequately representing a higher order of reality than the system which we call matter of fact. It is by no means certain that the analogy of dreams (for, of course, it is only an analogy) makes against mysticism. The fact of dreams makes us familiar with the conception of different grades and orders of reality. We do not live always in the same world. There are breaches of continuity, and even contradictions, in our experience, which may cause us to doubt whether our normal states are absolutely trustworthy. We pass from one state to another without change of place. May there not be other and higher orders of reality into which some persons have entered in the same manner? Philosophers have found radical contradictions in some of the conceptions which form the very warp

and woof of our thought—time, space, and
the self. May not these contradictions be
an indication that the world of common-sense
is itself a dream rather than reality—a system,
that is, which would appear unsubstantial if
viewed from the standpoint of a higher reality?

It must be remembered that the application
of the standard of naive sensationism to
spiritual things is as fatal to art and poetry
as to religion. We have no single weighing-
machine for gauging the amount of substance
in every kind of experience. The world as
projected by the ethical or the æsthetic
faculties has as good a right to claim reality
as that which the natural sciences reveal to us.
No science which deals with one aspect of
reality (as molecular physics deals with the
relations which atoms, if there were such
things, would hold to each other) exhausts
what may be truly said about things. Moreover, in the higher spheres of experience
especially, a man sees what it is in him to
see, not all that is there to see. And he can
only describe what he sees symbolically and
inadequately. Language, which was framed

to express daily needs and common ideas, breaks down when it is called upon to describe the deeper experiences of the soul. It struggles to find similes for what cannot be said directly. If the poet, and sometimes the artist—William Blake, for instance—are driven to use strange symbols to express their ideas, personifying the forces of nature and hunting everywhere for metaphors and analogies, even more must this be so with the religious genius. To him the vision is very real, so real that (as I have said) it possesses him rather than is possessed by him; but it is not given in words, and cannot be adequately rendered by words.

The oft-repeated complaint of the mystics, that they cannot express what they have seen, is not to be ridiculed. Dante, who knew both the psychology of the schools and the psychology of the saints, shows us that so it must be :—

> " E vidi cose che redire
> Nè sa nè può qual di lassù discende ;
> Perchè, appresando se al suo disire,
> Nostro intelletto si profonda tanto,
> Che retro la memoria non può ire."[1]

---

[1] *Paradiso* i.

And again :—

> "Qual e colui che somniando vede,
> E dopo il sogno la passione impressa
> Rimane, e l'altro alla mente non riede,
> Cotal son io, che quasi tutta cessa
> Mia visione, ed ancor mi distilla
> Nel cuor lo dolce che nacque da essa." [1]

If we understand what the mystic tells us, it is largely because we have experienced something of the same kind ourselves, and are able by sympathy to fill up for ourselves what words and images only give in a blurred and dim picture. The same is true of art also. No one, I think, would enjoy or appreciate a fine sea-picture if he had never seen the sea. The finest lyric poetry is tedious to those whose emotional nature is undeveloped.

The parallel between the artistic and the religious representation of things is very significant. They are akin in that both are essentially unselfish. The selfish man remembers and observes only what has served or baffled him. But art is the wide world's memory of things. It values the things of

---

[1] *Paradiso* xxxiii.

experience according as they are good or bad ; that is, according as they fulfil their proper end or not. Even so religion, which is the negation of selfishness, views things *sub specie aeternitatis*, and not according as they cause pleasure or pain to ourselves. But the religious representation of reality is subject to more stringent restrictions than the artistic, in that, since the main end of art is *enjoyment*, there is an element of play, of conscious illusion, in its productions. Art accepts gladly its own limitations. But there is no element of play in religious symbolism. The religious attitude is one of the highest conceivable seriousness. Its subject is reality in the final and highest sense. It can acknowledge its own imperfection, but not acquiesce in its illusions. It reverences its symbols while admitting their inadequacy. We know that they are not creations of our fancy, like artistic symbols, but the spontaneous projections of a deeper faculty which we dare not trifle with. Hence comes that reluctance to subject religious symbols to rationalistic tests, which we observe everywhere in human history. If we remember

this peculiar attitude of the religious consciousness towards symbolism, we shall find a ready
solution of one of the apparent inconsistencies
in mystical thought, which even a sympathetic
critic of mysticism such as Royce regards as
a fundamental contradiction. I mean the fact
that mysticism, the *differentia* of which is the
craving for *immediacy* in the knowledge or
vision of God, is at the same time intimately
associated with symbolism. Mysticism has
no love for symbols that are merely symbols
—"loose types of things through all degrees."
It rests in no half-lights ; it longs to tear the
heart out of every experience. It longs to
dive into the hidden reality behind phenomena,
and, in so far as it succeeds, it treats the
phenomena as symbols. But the temper which
makes playthings of symbols—which finds an
æsthetic or fanciful pleasure in them—is above
all things alien to it.

But we are likely to hear the following
objection. Before attributing to mystical
intuitions or visions an even higher authority
than belongs to the reflections of the
philosopher or the imagination of the poet,

should we not remember that recent investigations have made it more than probable that all such experiences are pathological, being invariably found to be associated with more or less morbid conditions of the mind or body? Was not St Paul, the mystic of the New Testament, probably an epileptic, and certainly a neurotic subject? Are not the records of monastic mysticism full of symptoms which are now known to indicate loss of mental balance? Nay, is it not probable that the religious experience is essentially of the nature of a self-induced trance, the empirical wisdom of the nations having discovered in the production of this trance one of the most efficacious means of stamping on the mind such suggestions as shall secure the triumph of the dearest wishes of the human heart? What evidence can be more conclusive than that notable mystics like Jacob Böhme admit that they induced their visions by what would now be called self-hypnotisation — gazing fixedly at a point of light shining through a keyhole, and the like?

Well, these objections are made by specialists,

and deserve to be treated with respect. But the real question is, whether our higher endowments are best interpreted from above or from below. Is their true nature to be found by enquiring what they grew out of, and with what physical conditions they are associated, or by enquiring what they may grow into, and to what regions of spiritual truth they may conduct us? The former is the method of pessimism. Lucretius, Swift, and Schopenhauer try to make the passion of love odious and contemptible in this way. The more a thing is good, the higher it has risen from its first state, and consequently the more it can be degraded by identifying it with its original forms. It is essentially the pessimistic method. Pessimism maintains that all human endeavour is futile, all progress illusory; that the attractiveness of physical or moral beauty is merely a bait by which Nature entices us to subserve her purposes to our own hurt; and that the mystics are persons who, by reason of their unstable nervous system, are more completely duped than their neighbours. But Christianity agrees with Aristotelianism in teaching that the nature of a thing is its ultimate potentiality of development. The tree is to be known by its fruits, not by its roots. Nor can the products of religious genius be discredited by pointing to the frail and suffering lives of their authors. We do not judge poetry in this way, though eccentricity has been common enough amongst poets. Even if it were true that religious genius appears only in an abnormal physical and mental constitution, that would not destroy the value of what the religious genius has revealed to us. Nature often gives with one hand what she takes away with the other. It is not the harmoniously developed men to whom the world owes most. But, in point of fact, the great saints have been no more eccentric than other men of exceptional gifts— I would even say, less so.

Our English saints have been very sane and sensible, even when most clearly belonging to the mystical type. Those whom I have chosen as specimens in these lectures, whether recluses, or philosophers, or poets, might have defied even a mad doctor to do his worst.

D

I am not altogether holding a brief for mysticism. It is a type of religion which no one would wish to see in possession of the whole field, and which is very liable to perversions. It cannot be an accident that it has been generally treated as the religion of pure *feeling*, and opposed to ethical theism on the one side, and to intellectual systems, such as absolute idealism, on the other. I have tried to show that the moral sense and the speculative faculty both have their mystical states, and that both types have, in point of fact, contributed to the literature and hagiology of mysticism. But, in spite of this, the trend of mysticism in the direction of pure feeling has been so marked, that the name is not likely to be readily given to piety of another type. In modern times, it will be said, the typical mystical divine is Schleiermacher, the founder of romanticism in theology. He opposed the intellectual idealism of Hegel, disparaging knowledge as of very subordinate importance to faith, and making faith to consist entirely of devout feeling. "The sum total of religion," he says, "is to feel that in its highest unity

all that moves us in feeling is one — to
feel, that is to say, that our being and
living is a being and living in and through
God."

And again he says that, in the religious
experience, "You become sense, and the
whole becomes object. Sense and object
mingle and unite, and then each returns to
its place, and the object rent from sense is
a perception, and you rent from the object
are, for yourselves, a feeling. It is this
earlier moment I mean, which you always
experience, yet never experience. The
phenomena of your life is just its constant
departure and return. It is scarcely in time
at all, so quickly does it pass ; it can
scarcely be described, so little does it
properly exist. Would that I could hold it
fast, and refer to it your commonest as well
as your highest activities. . . . It is the
first contact of the universal life with the
individual. . . . It is immediate, raised above
all error and misunderstanding. You lie
directly on the bosom of the infinite world.
In that moment you are its soul. Through

one part of your nature you feel, as your own, all its powers and its endless life. In this way every living original movement in your life is first conceived. It is the source of every religious emotion."

This extract from Schleiermacher would, I think, be very widely accepted as typical mystical teaching. The revelation of God is said to be given in immediate feeling, and in no other way. That this account of religious experience is one-sided and inadequate almost all would admit; does the admission condemn mysticism, or not?

I do not like the quasi-personification of our faculties which is so common in discussions on the borderland between metaphysics and psychology. Men champion the cause of the Will, or the Intellect, or the Feeling, as if they were three rival powers contending for the supremacy over our lives. The unity of our personality is often lost sight of. Still, the classification is convenient for certain purposes, and we may use it if we always remember that it involves us in unreal abstractions. With this caution, we may say that the religious consciousness begins as pure feeling. It begins with a lower kind of immediacy, which I should express in religious phraseology by saying that it begins with God's self-revealing presence in our consciousness. God lends us a portion of His eternal life, that we may at length make it our own. But it can only become our own by passing for a while quite out of the sphere of immediate perception. Feeling must pass into will. In so passing it does not cease to be feeling, but becomes conscious of itself as feeling. And Will, when it becomes conscious of itself as will, passes into intelligence, without ceasing to be will. The reconciling principle between will and intelligence or knowledge is love, as has been recently well shown by McTaggart (*Studies in Hegelian Dialectic*). This corresponds with the thesis of some mystical theologians, that what they call the "mixed" state is higher than contemplation, being the perfect union of contemplation and action. But this "intellectual love of God," as Spinoza called it, is a reversion, on a much higher plane, to the pure feeling, or immediacy, with which we said religion begins. The religious experience has described a full circle, and has entered into the inheritance which was shown to it, as its own, at the beginning of its course. "The highest and lowest things are simple," says Proclus the Neo-Platonist; "the intermediate are complex."

The danger to which the mystics have often fallen victims is the temptation to clutch at the fruition of the spiritual union before they have gone through the toilsome preparation and discipline of the will and intellect. They have tried to live throughout in the pleasant region of devout feeling. The result of this impatience is sometimes that the intellect is sacrificed or remains outside the religious life. In such cases there is no check upon superstitious beliefs, which often take the form of fantastic theosophy or magic; and no check upon such excesses of emotionalism as are frequently witnessed at religious revivals. Sometimes it is the ethical faculty which is starved. This very serious omission has in history issued in two perversions — anti-

nomianism and quietism. The former teaches
that he who is led by the Spirit can do no
wrong, or that the sins of the body cannot
stain the soul. The latter teaches that we
can "hearken what the Lord God will say
concerning us" most satisfactorily if we sit
with folded arms. It must be admitted that
those schools of philosophy which are most
in sympathy with mysticism have been on the
whole ethically weak. The classical form of
mystical philosophy is Oriental pantheism,
which by obliterating all outlines makes all
things equally divine, and leaves no room
for distinctions between right and wrong.
Emerson has drunk deeply of this intoxicating
draught of self-deification :—

> "There is no great and no small
>   To the soul that maketh all :
>   Where it cometh, all things are,
>   And it cometh everywhere.

> "I am the owner of the sphere,
>   Of the seven stars and the solar year,
>   Of Cæsar's hand, and Plato's brain,
>   Of Lord Christ's heart, and Shakespeare's strain."

Most mystical philosophers have been
determinists. Plotinus cannot be considered

an exception; and the systems of Spinoza
and Hegel are found unsatisfactorily by all
who lay much stress on human volition.
Hence perhaps comes the extreme dislike of
mysticism expressed by many ethical theists,
especially by the German Ritschlians. A
form of religion which tends to mix up man
and God, to break down the rigid limits of
individuality, and to make evil an unreal
appearance, must, they think, be morally
injurious. But there is no real inconsistency
between mysticism and the strictest ethics, or
the keenest speculation. Mysticism repudiates
intellectualism, not intellect, moralism, not
morality. It insists, no doubt, on personal
inspiration as the *source* of religion. As
Emerson says—

"This communication is an influx of the
Divine mind into our mind. It is an ebb of
the individual rivulet before the flowing surges
of the sea of life. . . . The character and
duration of this enthusiasm varies with the
state of the individual, from an ecstasy and
trance and prophetic inspiration, to the faintest
glow of virtuous emotion, in which form it

warms, like our household fires, all the families
and associations of men, and makes society
possible."

But this glow rapidly becomes extinct unless
it kindles a flame in the will and intellect.
All mysticism which seeks its life in inactive
contemplation only, is a failure. The God
who "worketh hitherto" is not to be found
or known by any who leave their practical
energies unused. Those who desire above
all things to feel and enjoy their power of
communion with God, are bound to remember
that our relation to God must be that of
finite and dependent beings. On one side
we have fellowship with the Father; on the
other we are very far removed and even
estranged from Him.

Does not this throw more light on that
feature in mystical literature which seems so
self-contradictory? I mean, the claim to
immediate contact with the Divine, combined
with a chart of spiritual progress representing
a very long ladder of ascent? Such is indeed
the course of the spiritual life. It is an
infinite progress *within* the sphere of Divine

E

love and knowledge.   And in its development it uses, and in using hallows, all our faculties.

In asking you, as I shall ask you, to listen to two lectures upon the older mystical literature in our language, I am not trying to interest you in dead theology.   There is a great deal of dead theology; most of it died at a very early age; some was alive for centuries and is now dead.   But the books of the great mystics do not die.   They may be forgotten, as the *Theologia Germanica* was forgotten; but so soon as they become known again, they are found to be very much alive. "A book only grows old," says Maeterlinck, "by reason of its anti-mysticism."

"Those books which vividly depict in some fashion or other the felt presence of the Divine and the Universal in human natures have a perennial charm, and are among the most precious of the treasures which the world will not willingly let die."[1]

I think you will be surprised at the freshness and modernity of the extracts which I shall read you next week and the week after

[1] Upton, *Hibbert Lectures*, 1893.

from the *Ancren Riwle*, Julian of Norwich, and Walter Hylton. Human nature is said to be much the same everywhere at the bottom. It is also so at the top. We need not trouble ourselves to ask, and we could seldom guess without asking, whether a paragraph describing the highest spiritual experiences was written in the Middle Ages or in modern times, in the north or south of Europe, by a Catholic or by a Protestant.

The fourth lecture I shall devote to the eighteenth-century divine, William Law, who from the seclusion of a remote village issued several treatises of a mystical type which are unsurpassed for robustness of thought and beauty of expression, in the sacred literature of our country.

In the two last lectures I shall take two poets — Wordsworth and Browning — as my subjects. The poets have been our most influential prophets and preachers in the nineteenth century; and it so happens that these two furnish us with the best possible examples of certain kinds of mystical thought and feeling.

Among such a variety of testimony, converging from many sides towards one central truth, most of my hearers should be able to find some message which they can take home to themselves. With all of us, the range of spiritual vision is extremely limited. We are like persons gazing at the moonlight on the sea. Every wave and wavelet reflects the light, but each spectator sees only one narrow silvery path, that which stretches to the horizon straight out from his own feet. Only those who lean entirely on external authority are likely to be disappointed with, and to disapprove of, *all* the mystics. And to them I will read a few wise words from a very eminent and thoughtful philosopher, the late Professor Wallace.

"In the Kingdom of God are many mansions; and while some are content, as it were, to live on tradition and authority, to believe on trust, to repose on the common strength, it is necessary that there should also be from time to time a few, a select number, who resolve, or rather are compelled by a necessity naturally laid upon them, to

see for themselves. Theirs also is faith;
but it is the faith of insight and of knowledge, the faith which is gnosis. Hard
things have been said of gnosis, and harder
things of gnosticism; but it cannot be too
clearly seen that gnosis is the very life
of the Church, the blood of religion. It is
the faith which is not merely hearsay and
dependence, but which really envisages the
unseen for itself. It does not believe *on* a
Person; it believes in and into Him: it
becomes, by an act at once voluntary and
impelled from without (as all human action
that is really entitled to that name) participant
with Him and through Him of a force of life
and conduct."

I have troubled you with no definitions of
mysticism. But when you have heard what
the authorities whom I have selected have
to say for themselves, I hope and think that
you will conclude that the shortest definition
which has ever been suggested is also one
of the best. Mysticism is the love of God.

LECTURE II

THE *ANCREN RIWLE* AND JULIAN OF NORWICH

THE life of the recluse is now seldom chosen and never respected. It is difficult for us to realise that it was once a career, and not the abdication of all careers. The professional saint almost disappeared from Northern Europe at or before the Reformation. In the earlier Middle Ages, however, his was a recognised manner of life which, however austere, did not at all condemn him who had chosen it to obscurity or contempt. The hermit becomes an important figure in Church history in the half century which followed the Decian persecution, when many thousands in Northern Africa alone fled to the deserts, renouncing all domestic and civic ties. In ecclesiastical circles, at any rate, it was the shortest road to a high reputation. Pilgrims who visited the caves and huts in which the hermits found shelter, spread far and wide accounts of their austerities and their miracles. They described how some lived in dried-up wells, others among the tombs, others on pillars. The macerations to which they subjected themselves — their abstinence from food, sleep, and ablutions — made them heroes at a time when mortification of the flesh was considered the highest virtue. They were consulted on problems of theology, and even on practical questions. This movement, one of the most difficult in history for moderns to comprehend, was on its saner side a great purity crusade, combined with a desire to cultivate to the utmost the spiritual life by sacrificing all else to it. To call the hermits selfish is a mistake. There is room for this kind of specialisation as well as for others. If the hermits "produced" nothing, in the economic sense, they consumed next to nothing; and even those who are most sceptical about the value of intercessory prayer may admit that the true saint, who can bring his example and influence to bear on the social life of his generation, is a useful member of the community.

It is true that we cannot regard the anchorite as the most perfect imitator of Jesus Christ. Our Master began His ministry at a marriage feast. He was continually reproached for practising no austerities in public, and for associating freely with all classes and with both sexes. Monkish ethics involved a violent distortion of the true Christian ideal. But now that eremitism in the Church has become an episode of past history, we may admit a partial justification for those who practised it, in the desire to bring to its highest perfection the faculty of spiritual vision — the contemplation of the light invisible. Their experiences illustrate the advantage as well as the defects of a highly specialised training.

In the Middle Ages, England was full of persons who in one form or another had taken religious vows. Besides the larger monasteries and convents, there were numerous "anchorages" for solitary women, some in the open country, but more in the vicinity of a church. The cell of the anchoress, which was often built against the church wall or in a churchyard, sometimes contained more than one apartment, for the recluse usually had one, or even two, servants to attend upon her. She herself never left the walls of her cell, which had no means of egress, except by the windows. Even the window which opened towards the outside was generally covered by a heavy curtain, and those who wished for an audience with the recluse would kneel before the window until she chose to draw back the screen.

The *Ancren Riwle*, a precious specimen of early English, was written for three anchoresses, sisters, who had retired from the world for pious exercises, and lived together with their domestic servants or lay sisters. They were not, it seems, connected with any religious community. They lived at Tarrant Kaines, Dorsetshire. The reputed author of the *Ancren Riwle* is Simon de Ghent, Archdeacon of Oxford in 1284, and Bishop of Salisbury 1297-1315. But the style is said to be earlier, and it is more probable that it was written by Bishop Poore, who was born and buried there. The author of the *Ancren Riwle* was certainly a learned man ; he quotes the Christian Fathers, and even Pagan poets,

F

such as Horace and Ovid.   His treatise is just
what it professes to be, a compendium of rules
and good advice for anchoresses.   It is not,
properly speaking, a document of mystical
theology, like the *Revelations* of Julian of
Norwich, or Hylton's *Scale of Perfection*,
which will presently engage our attention.
But it is a very interesting treatise in itself,
and throws so much light on the conditions
under which these recluses lived and saw
their visions, that it will not be out of place
to give you some account of its contents, before
proceeding to the still more attractive work
of Julian, another anchoress.

The book is divided into eight sections,
entitled (i) On Devotional Exercises ; (ii) On
the Government of the Senses in keeping the
Heart ; (iii) Moral Lessons and Examples ;
(iv) Temptations and Means to avoid them ;
(v) On Confession ; (vi) On Penance and
Amendment ; (vii) On Love or Charity ;
(viii) On Domestic and Social Duties.

The author begins by saying : " My dear
sisters, you have asked me for a Rule.   But
I will only give you two rules.   One rules the

heart, and makes it even and smooth, without
any knot or scar of evil. This is charity out
of a pure heart, and love unfeigned. The
other is all external. It is bodily exercise or
discipline, which, the apostle says, profiteth
little. This rule is only to serve the other.
The rule of love is as lady, the rule of
discipline as handmaid. The rule of love is
always the same, the rule of discipline may be
changed and varied.

"If you are asked to what order you belong,
say, 'The Order of St James.' For it is
St James who wrote: 'Pure religion and
undefiled before God and the Father is this,
to visit the fatherless and widows in their
affliction, and to keep oneself unspotted from
the world.'" Then follow directions for daily
devotions. "On waking say, 'In the name
of the Father and of the Son and of the Holy
Ghost,'" followed by the *Veni Creator*, kneel-
ing on your beds. Many offices are enjoined
during the day, including, it must be owned,
a terrible amount of vain repetition, especially
of Paternosters.

The ancient prayer which they are ordered

to say at the Holy Communion is remarkable for the spiritual and unsuperstitious doctrine of the Eucharist which it implies : " Grant, we beseech thee, almighty God, that Him whom we see darkly, and under a different form, and on whom we feed sacramentally on earth, we may see face to face, and may be thought worthy to enjoy Him truly and really as He is in heaven, through the same Jesus Christ our Lord."

The chapter on the " Guard of the Senses " contains some amusing admonitions. The young ladies are cautioned severely against looking out of the parlour window, " like the staring anchoresses." And they are not to be always chattering with visitors, " like the cackling anchoresses" (*kakelinde ancren*). Silence is always to be observed at meals, and throughout Friday, and during Holy Week. It is permissible, however, to say " a few words " to your maid, during silent times. But talking is a snare. " More slayeth word than sword."

Gossip was evidently a temptation to the recluse. " People say," writes our author, "that an anchoress has always a magpie to chatter to her; so that men have a proverb: 'From miln and market, from smithy and nunnery, men bring tidings.' Christ knows, this is a sad tale."

Our Lord's words, "Foxes have holes, and birds of the air have nests," may be allegorically applied to true and false anchoresses. "The true anchoresses are indeed birds of heaven, that fly aloft and sit on the green boughs singing merrily. That is, they meditate enraptured upon the blessedness of heaven that never fadeth and is ever green. A bird, however, sometimes alighteth on earth to seek food, but never feels secure there, and often turns herself about," on her guard against danger. Even so should the anchoress be wary when she is obliged to busy herself with earthly things. This pretty comparison has been also made use of by a French poet:—

"Soyons comme l'oiseau, posé pour un instant
   Sur des rameaux trop frêles;
Qui sent ployer la branche, et qui chante pourtant,
   Sachant qu' il a des ailes."

The seven deadly sins are then compared
to animals, pride to the lion, envy to the
serpent, and so forth. The noxious beasts
all have "whelps" — seven, twelve, or six
particular vices which all belong to the
deadly sin in question. The best worth
quoting of these somewhat arbitrary classi-
fications is the paragraph about *accidie*, that
besetting sin of the cloister :—

"The bear of heavy sloth hath these whelps.
Torpor is the first—that is, a lukewarm heart.
Next is pusillanimity, which is too faint-
hearted and too reluctant withal to under-
take any high thing in hope of God's help and
trust in His grace. The third is dullness of
heart. Who doeth good, but with a dead and
sluggish heart, he hath this whelp. Fourth
is idleness. Whoso stands still, doing no
good at all, he hath this whelp. Fifth is a
grudging and grumbling heart. Sixth is
sorrow for anything except sin. Seventh is
negligence in saying or doing or providing
or remembering or taking care. The eighth
is despair, the grimmest bear's whelp of
all, which cheweth and wasteth God's mild

kindness and much mercy and boundless grace."

The sow of greediness and her pigs are very briefly disposed of, "for I am nought afeard, my beloved sisters, that ye feed them."

There is a remarkable passage about the consolations which an anchoress experiences at first, but which she must not expect to enjoy always. This caution, which we find in almost all who have written with intimate knowledge about the life of devotion, is psychologically and practically of great interest. "An anchoress thinks [beforehand] that she shall be most strongly tempted in the first twelve months. Nay, it is not so. In the first years, it is nothing but ball-play." "In the beginning it is only courtship, to draw you into love." Afterwards, you must expect to be treated with "less forbearance," but "in the end cometh great joy."

The exhortation to sisterly affection is written with great delicacy, and a sort of quaint tenderness which is very charming.

"My dear sisters, let your dear noses

always be turned to each other with sweet love, fair semblance, and with sweet cheer, that ye may be ever with oneness of one heart and of one will, united together. While you are united, the fiend cannot harm you. . . . And if the fiend blow up any resentment between you, which may Jesus Christ forbid, until it is appeased none ought to receive Jesus Christ's flesh and blood. . . . But let each send word to the other, that she hath humbly asked her forgiveness, as if she were present."

We obtain little glimpses into the minor troubles and arrangements of the household when we read special admonitions like the following : "Be glad in your hearts if ye suffer insolence from Slurry the cook's knave, who washes the dishes in the kitchen." "My dear sisters, ye shall have no beast but one cat."

Lastly, the good man is distressed to find his spiritual daughters treating themselves too hardly. "Dear sisters, your meat and drink have seemed to me less than I would have it." He forbids them to wear hedgehog skins as a discipline, or iron or haircloth, and to beat themselves with leathern thongs, or with a leaded lash, or with holly or briars till the blood comes, at least without leave from their confessor. Their clothes are to be warm and well made, "and as many as you need, both for bed and back." They are allowed to wash, we are glad to find, "as often as you please."

Such are the rules and exhortations drawn up for three young ladies in the early part (probably) of the thirteenth century. They will help us to realise the kind of life lived by the numerous female recluses belonging to the upper and middle classes, in the Middle Ages. For our purposes the most interesting and important of these ladies is Julian of Norwich, the author of one of the most precious gems of mediæval sacred literature. To her life and revelations I now turn.

In Blomefield's History of Norfolk (1768) we read :—

"In the east part of the churchyard [of the old church of St Julian in the parish of Conisford, near Norwich] stood an anchorage in which an anchoress or recluse dwelt till the dissolution, when the house was demolished, though the foundations may still be seen. In 1393 Lady Julian, the ankeress here, was a strict recluse, and had two servants to attend her in her old age. In 1472 Dame Agnes was recluse here; in 1481 Dame Elizabeth Scott; in 1510 Lady Elizabeth; in 1524 Dame Agnes Edrygge."

"The little church of St Julian" (says Miss Warrack, whose beautiful edition of Julian's *Revelations* should be in the hands of all who are interested in our present subject) "still keeps from Norman times its dark round tower of flint rubble, and still there are traces about its foundation of the anchorage built against its south-eastern wall." The church was assigned by King Stephen to the nuns of Carrow, a small Benedictine house, the inmates of which in the fifteenth century conducted a fashionable girls' school.

The Lady Julian (the prefix was commonly given by courtesy to recluses of gentle birth) was probably a Benedictine nun belonging to this convent. She was thirty years old when in May 1373 the revelation was made to her which she afterwards recorded in narrative form. She must have lived to an extraordinary age, if we may trust the title, written by a contemporary on an old vellum manuscript of the *Visions*. "Here is a vision showed by the goodness of God to a devout woman; and her name is Julian, that is recluse at Norwich, and yet is on life, Anno Domini 1442." Nothing is else known about her, except from the *Visions* themselves. The attempt to identify her with a Lady Julian Lampet, of Carrow Abbey, who appears to have died about 1480, is manifestly impossible.

Julian describes herself as "a simple creature that could no letter." Whatever may have been the state of her education at the time when she saw the Visions, she was far from being an illiterate person when she wrote them down. Phrases like "after this I saw God in a point," show some acquaintance with the theological learning of the time. The style of the narrative is very simple, but by no means lacking in literary skill.

The description of the revelations made to
her at the age of thirty is one of the most attractive documents of mysticism, owing to the combination of fine qualities shown by the author.
Her unaffected humility is not more pronounced
than her simple desire to know the truth.   Her
love to God and man is expressed in such
sentences as : "What may make me more to
love mine even Christen (fellow Christians)
than to see in God that He loveth all that
shall be saved as it were all one soul?" and
by her "desire to learn assuredly as to a
certain creature that I loved, if it should
continue in good living." Particularly pleas-
ing is her thoroughly sane estimate of the
favours which God had bestowed upon her.
"It was not showed me that God loved me
better than the least soul that was in grace ;
for I am certain that there be many that never
had any showing nor sight, but of the common
teaching of Holy Church, that love God better
than I." If we contrast Julian's *Revelations*
with the *Visions* of the Nun Gertrude, a
paltry record of sickly compliments and semi-
erotic endearments, we shall realise how far

the English saint rises above her more
honoured sister. It does not seem that her
happy nature was much assailed by the
common temptation of the cloister — gloom
and sloth. She speaks of "sloth and losing
of time" as "the beginning of sin, as to my
sight," "especially to the creatures who have
given themselves to serve our Lord with
inward beholding of His blessed goodness";
but there is no personal confession here.

Her own account of her *Visions* is very
interesting. It is true that it was not written
for some years after the event, and that to
describe such an experience after a lapse of
time is as difficult as to paint a sunset from
memory. But there can be no question that
Julian tells the truth to the best of her
ability. Absolute candour is a feature of the
whole narrative; and modern psychology
must recognise the scientific accuracy of her
description of the conditions under which the
visions occurred. Julian had prayed for three
gifts from God. The first was that she might
bear the Passion of Christ in mind. The
second was that she might have a bodily

sickness at thirty years of age; "the third was to have, of God's gift, three wounds." As to the first, she "thought she had some feeling," but she desired, if possible, a "bodily sight" of Christ upon the Cross, to quicken her sympathies, that she might be "one of His lovers and suffer with Him." "Other sight nor shewing of God, desired I never none, till the soul were disparted from the body." The sickness she desired to be as severe and painful as might be, short of death, that after it she might be purged by the mercy of God, and live to God more because of that sickness. These two petitions Julian made "with a condition"—"if it be Thy will that I have it." But the "three wounds"—namely, the wounds of very contrition, of kind (*i.e.* natural) compassion, and of wilful (*i.e.* purposeful, steadfast) longing toward God—she prayed for absolutely, knowing the request to be in accordance with the will of God.

Her prayer for a severe sickness at the age of thirty was fulfilled to the letter. After a sharp attack, which lasted three days, she

received the last rites of the church and
"languored forth" between life and death
for two days afterwards. "Being in youth
as yet, I thought it great sorrow to die,"
she says simply; but she was fully resigned,
and said to herself: "Good Lord, may my
living no longer be to Thy worship." What
follows is so important a document on the
physical conditions which may precede trance
that I will give it in her own words (from
Miss Warrack's edition, p. 6):—

"Thus I dured till day, and by then my body
was dead from the middle downwards, as to my
feeling. Then was I minded to be set upright,
backward leaning, with help—for to have more
freedom of my heart to be at God's will, and
thinking on God while my life would last. My
Curate was sent for to be at my ending, and
by that time when he came I had set my eyes,
and might not speak. He set the Cross before
my face and said: 'I have brought thee the
image of thy Maker and Saviour: look there-
upon and comfort thee therewith.' Methought
I was well (*i.e.* as it was), for my eyes were
set uprightward unto Heaven, where I trusted

to come by the mercy of God; but nevertheless I assented to set my eyes on the face
of the Crucifix, if I might, and so I did. For
methought I might no longer dure to look even-
forth than right up. After this my sight began
to fail, and it was all dark about me in the
chamber as if it had been night, save in the
image of the Cross, whereon I beheld a
common light; and I wist not how. All that
was beside the Cross was of horror to me, as
if it had been greatly occupied by the fiends.
After this the over part of my body began to
die, so far forth that scarcely I had any feeling,
with shortness of breath. And then I weened
in sooth to have passed. And in this suddenly
all my pain was taken from me, and I was as
whole (and specially in the upper part of my
body) as ever I was afore. I marvelled at this
sudden change, for methought it was a privy
working of God, and not of nature. And yet
by the feeling of this ease I trusted never the
more to live; nor was the feeling of this ease
any full ease unto me; for methought I had
liefer have been delivered from this world.
Then came suddenly to my mind that I

should desire the second wound of our Lord's gracious gift; that my body might be fulfilled with mind and feeling of His blessed Passion. For I would that His pains were my pains, with compassion and afterward longing to God. But in this I desired never bodily sight nor shewing of God, but compassion such as a kindred soul might have with our Lord Jesus, that for love would be a mortal man; and therefore I desired to suffer with Him.

"In this moment suddenly I saw the red blood trickle down from under the garland hot and freshly and right plenteously, as it were in the time of His Passion, when the garland of thorns was pressed on His blessed head. I conceived truly and mightily that it was Himself showed it me, without any mean."

In this very interesting and careful description of the beginning of her visions, we should note especially the state of hypnotism induced by steadily gazing at the Crucifix, on which also her thoughts were fixed with ardent longing. To fix the eyes steadily on

H

one object seems to be almost a necessary
condition of this kind of trance. Before
describing the substance of her visions, it
may be well to collect other passages which
throw light on her psychical state.

Among her early visions on this occasion
was one of a landscape—a sea-shore, with
hills and valleys, and ground covered with
moss. This seemed to her so low and little
and simple, that she was some time in doubt
"whether it was a shewing." Then more light
was vouchsafed to her, but the pictorial image
seems to have passed into something quite
different. Another passage shows that she
was not in a cataleptic state. For when she
was shown a vision of Our Lord scorning the
malice and setting at nought the "unmight"
of the foul fiend, she "laughed mightily, and
that made them to laugh that were about
me, and their laughing was a pleasure to
me." She is careful to add that she saw
Christ mocking the devil "by leading of mine
understanding; that is to say, it was an
inward shewing of verity, without change of
look." "I saw not Christ laugh." A third

passage which is worth our attention describes
how she asked for a special revelation about
the spiritual condition of one who was dear
to her, which was not granted. The answer
which came to her was : "Take it generally,
and behold the graciousness of the Lord God
as He sheweth to thee; for it is more
worship to God to behold Him in all than
in any special thing." It is also remarkable
that she draws distinctions as to the manner of
her visions. "Our courteous Lord answered
in shewing full mightily a wonderful example
of the Lord that hath a servant : which sight
was shewed doubly in the Lord and doubly
in the servant; the one part was shewed
spiritually in bodily likeness, and the other
part was shewed more spiritually, without
bodily likeness." Another vision she almost
recognises to have been an ordinary nightmare.
"In my sleep, methought the fiend set him
on my throat, putting forth a visage full
near my face, like a young man's, and it
was long and wondrous lean : I never saw
none such. This horrible shewing was made
sleeping, and so was none other." Later on

she says very definitely: "All the blessed
teaching of our Lord was shewed by three
parts; that it is say, by bodily sight, and
by word formed in mine understanding, and
by spiritual sight. For the bodily sight, I
have said as I saw, as truly as I can; and
for the words, I have said them right as our
Lord shewed them to me; and for the
spiritual sight, I have told some deal, but
I may never fully tell it." The book ends
with an explanation of the long interval
between the visions and the writing of the
book. "From the time that it was shewed
I desired oftentimes to witten what was our
Lord's meaning. And fifteen years after,
and more, I was answered in ghostly understanding, saying thus: 'Would'st thou learn
thy Lord's meaning in this thing? Learn
it well. Love was His meaning.'" Julian
evidently believes that she has preserved in
memory the substance of the visions exactly
as they occurred to her fifteen years earlier;
it is only the "meaning" that was revealed
later. Her readers can only feel assured of
the absolute candour of her recital. Signs

of rhetorical ornament and literary furbishing are hardly traceable in these pages.

Those who wish to appreciate Julian of Norwich must read her little book for themselves. Here I can only call attention to some prominent characteristics.

Julian is one of the *happy* saints. Like the Franciscans, who held it a point of honour that the bridegrooms of my lady Poverty must never be melancholy, she finds good everywhere, and believes that God means us to be happy. "Marvellous and solemn is the place where the Lord dwelleth, and therefore He willeth that we readily entenden to His gracious teaching, more rejoicing in His whole love than sorrowing in our often fallings. For it is the most worship to Him of anything that we may do, that we live gladly and merrily, for His love, in our penance. For He beholdeth us so tenderly that He seeth all our living a penance. Nature's longing . . . is our natural penance —the highest, as to my sight. For this penance cometh never from us till we be fulfilled, when we shall have Him to our meed. And therefore He willeth that we set our hearts in the overpassing, that is to say, from the pain that we feel into the bliss that we trust." It is the enemy of our souls who maketh us to feel false dread, so that we are afraid to appear before "our courteous Lord." "For Jesus is our blessed Friend, and it is His will and counsel that we hold us with Him, and fasten us to Him homely evermore, in what state soever we be; for whether we are foul or clean, we are all one in His loving." Julian does not wish us to be implacable against ourselves. For "as God forgiveth our sin after we repent us, right so willeth He that we forgive our sin, as anent our unskilful (=useless) heaviness and our doubtful dreads." And in the vision of the Master and Servant, she says: "The most mischief that I saw him (the servant) in, was failing of comfort; for he could not turn his face to look upon his loving Lord, which was to him full near; in whom is full comfort; but as a man that was feeble and unwise for the time, he turned his mind to his feeling and endured his woe." The optimistic refrain : " All shall be well, and all shall be well, and all manner of thing shall be well," is the keynote of much of the book. It is caught up again in the concluding paragraphs. " Therefore when the doom is given, and we be all brought up above, then shall we clearly see in God the secret things which be now hid to us. Then shall none of us be stirred to say in any wise : ' Lord, if it had been thus, then it had been full well ; ' but we shall say all with one voice : ' Lord, blessed mote Thou be, for it is thus : it is well ; ' and now see we verily that all thing is done as it was then ordained before that anything was made." Not that sin is ignored by Julian. " In the third shewing, when I saw that God doeth all that is done, I saw no sin ; and then I saw that all is well. But when God shewed me for sin, then said He : ' All shall be well.' "

The attitude of a mystical writer in presence of the evil that is in the world is an important test how far we may regard him as a trustworthy guide. For of all the charges that have been brought against the

mystics, perhaps none is more possible to
justify than the accusation that they have an
inadequate sense of the havoc wrought by
sin. Julian does not solve the problem of
evil for us : but her words about it are true
and beautiful. " I stood," she says, " beholding
things general, troublously and mourning,
saying thus to our Lord, with full great
dread : 'Ah, good Lord, how might all be
well, for the great hurt that is come by sin
to the creature?' And here I desired, so far
as I durst, to have some more open declaring
whereby I might be eased in this matter."
The answer which she then received was
that the Fall of Man had been atoned for
by the death of Christ; "and since I have
made well the most harm, it is my will that
thou know thereby that I shall make well all
that is less." But the "making all things
well" is one of the works of our Lord God
that are yet to come. "There is a deed
which the blessed Trinity shall do in the last
day, but when the deed shall be, and how
it shall be done, is unknown of all creatures
that are beneath Christ, and shall be till

when it is done." Julian thus professes to have no revelation on this subject. And yet she shares the essentially optimistic conviction which we shall find to hold a still more central position in Browning's poetry, and which may also be found in St Augustine, that every stumbling-block may by God's grace be turned into a stepping-stone, so that our sins, in being conquered, may bring us nearer to God. "God shewed me," she says, "that sin shall be no shame to a man, but worship. For just as to every sin is answering a pain by truth, right so, for every sin, to the same soul is given a bliss by love. As diverse sins are punished with diverse pains according as they be grievous, right so shall they be rewarded with diverse joys in heaven according as they have been painful and sorrowful to the soul on earth." When the soul is healed, "his wounds are seen before God not as wounds but as worships. . . . So shall shame be turned to worship and more joy." "For grace worketh our dreadful failing into plenteous, endless solace; and grace worketh our shameful falling into high,

I

worshipful rising; and grace worketh our sorrowful dying into holy, blissful life."

In one curious chapter she distinctly raises the problem as to how a man who is partaker of the Divine nature, made in the image of God, and consisting essentially of a " Nature-Substance," which is ever kept one in Him whole and safe without end, can ever be worthy of blame and wrath. The truth on this difficult matter was " full mistily shewed " to her; but she thinks that we ought to distinguish between our " Nature-Substance," which is unstained by sin, and our " Sense-Soul," which, " as Holy Church teacheth," is guilty. Julian is not a metaphysician, and we need not go more deeply into the speculations with which she here shows some acquaintance. The doctrine of the impeccability of the higher Self is Neo-Platonic, and carries with it a whole system of philosophy and ethics.

Her gentle soul was much troubled at the notion of God's wrath. " Methought that to a soul whose meaning and desire is to love, the wrath of God was harder than any other pain, and therefore I took that the

forgiveness of this wrath should be one of the
principal points of His mercy. But for nought
that I might behold and desire I could not
see this." "I saw no wrath but on man's
part; and that forgiveth He in us. For
wrath is nought else but a frowardness and
contrariness to peace and love; and either it
cometh of failing of might, or of failing of
wisdom, or of failing of goodness, which
failing is not in God but on our part." "To
the soul that of His special grace seeth so
far into the high, marvellous goodness of
God, and seeth that we are endlessly oned
to Him in love, it is the most impossible
that may be, that God should be wroth. For
wrath and friendship be two contraries." "In
sooth, as to my sight, if God might be wroth
for a touch, we should never have life nor
place nor being."

Julian says that God was immediately
revealed to her, "in part," in three of his
attributes, "in which the strength and effect
of all the revelation standeth." These
attributes are Life, Love, and Light. "These
properties were in one Goodness." In the

Gospel and First Epistle of St John these
are the three attributes under which God
is immediately revealed, and so it has been
throughout the history of mystical theology.
Julian, however, forsakes the usual order,
which is Life, Light, Love. The Jacob's
ladder by which the mystic hopes to ascend
to heaven begins, as we shall see in the next
lecture, with external and internal discipline.
Light or illumination is the second stage, and
love is the crown and consummation. Of this
Julian is well aware, for, in the next chapter
she says : " The light is Charity . . . Charity
keepeth us in Faith and Hope, and Hope
leadeth us to Charity. And in the end all
shall be Charity. I had three manners of understanding this Light, Charity. The first is
Charity unmade ; the second is Charity made ;
and the third is Charity given. Charity unmade is God : Charity made is our soul in
God : and Charity given is virtue. And that
is a precious gift of working in which we
love God, for Himself ; and ourselves in God ;
and that which God loveth, for God." In
the previous chapter she desires to regard

the whole path of the just as a shining light, which shineth more and more unto the perfect day; and so she puts Light third. The concluding words of this chapter are among the most beautiful in the book. "And at the end of woe suddenly our eyes shall be opened, and in clearness of light our sight shall be full; which Light is God, our Maker and Holy Ghost, in Christ Jesus our Saviour. Thus I saw and understood that our faith is our light in our night; which light is God, our endless day."

We cannot leave Julian without some notice of the more distinctively mystical teaching which we find in her book. It is well known that most mystics lay great stress on what is called the *negative* road, in which the aim is to lose or throw away all human and finite knowledge, desire, and affection, in order that they may be found again, transmuted into something more Divine, in God. Julian is not a stranger to this method. "It needeth us," she says, "to know the littleness of the creatures, and to *noughten* all thing that is made, for to love and have God that is unmade." "If I ask anything that is less" than God, "ever me wanteth." And yet "the creatures" are made and loved and kept in being by God; they must not be despised. Only in all our use of them there is and must ever be something lacking; true bliss can only be ours when there is "right nought" between us and our Lord.

Another mystical doctrine, already touched upon in this lecture, is, that at the centre of our soul there is a pure spark of the Divine life, which always resists evil and remains in union with the central fire of Divine life and light, unless indeed the soul is utterly lost. "I saw and understood full surely that in every soul that shall be saved is a godly will that never assented unto sin, nor ever shall; which will is so good that it may never will evil, but evermore continually it willeth good and worketh good in the sight of God." It is through this godly will that we shall at last be united to God, though, she is careful to add, the redemption of mankind by Jesus Christ is "needful and speedful in everything, as Holy Church in our faith us teacheth."

Man's body, she thinks, was made of clay:
that is, of materials gathered from bodily
things; but his soul was made of nought,
and therefore has a natural affinity to the
unmade substance of God's nature. "High
understanding it is, inwardly to see and know
that God, which is our Maker, dwelleth in
our soul; and a higher understanding it is,
inwardly to see and know that our soul, which
is made, dwelleth in God's substance." "I
saw no difference between God and our
Substance, but as it were all God; and yet
mine understanding took that our Substance
is in God; that is to say, that God is God,
and our Substance is a creature in God. For
the almighty Truth of the Trinity is our
Father, for He made us and keepeth us in
Him; and the deep Wisdom of the Trinity
is our Mother, in whom we are all enclosed;
the high Goodness of the Trinity is our Lord,
in whom we are enclosed, and He in us."
"Our faith is a virtue that cometh of our
Nature-Substance into our Sense-Soul by the
Holy Ghost; in which all our virtues come
to us; for without that no man may receive

virtue." In other place she assigns to faith
a triple origin. "Our faith cometh of the
natural love of our soul, and of the clear
light of our reason, and of the steadfast mind
which we have of God in our first making."
This is a very remarkable sentence, a profound analysis of the foundations of belief.
Faith is an activity of our whole personality :
it stands, as Julian says, on the natural love
of our soul, our affections; on the clear
light of our reason; and on the steadfast
mind, or will, which we have of God. Perfect
faith involves the harmonious exercise of all
parts of our complex nature. A still more
remarkable paragraph follows, in which she
insists that the indwelling presence of God
is not confined to the highest part of our
nature, which she calls our Substance. God
cometh also in our "sensuality"—that part
of our nature which is the seat of the bodily
senses; "to this seat He cometh, and shall
never remove" from it. "All the gifts that
God may give the creatures, He hath given
to His Son Jesus for us : which gifts He,
dwelling in us, hath enclosed in Him until

the time that we be waxen and grown—our soul with our body and our body with our soul, *either of them taking help of other*, till we be brought up unto stature, as nature worketh. And then in the ground of nature, with working of mercy, the Holy Ghost graciously inspireth into us gifts leading to endless life." "And thus was my understanding led of God, to see in Him and understand, that our soul is made - Trinity, like to the unmade blissful Trinity, known and loved from without beginning, and in the making oned to the Maker. This sight was full sweet and marvellous to behold, peaceable, restful, sure, and delectable."

In this passage, the "made-Trinity" of which our soul consists reminds us strongly of the Neo-Platonic Trinity of Soul, Intelligence, and the Absolute One or Good, which are all, according to that philosophy, represented in the nature of man. But Julian's "Trinity" are the Truth that seeth God, the Wisdom that beholdeth God, and the Love that delighteth in God. These correspond to the attributes of the Father, the Son, and the

K

Holy Ghost respectively. The sentence about
body and soul "either taking help of the
other" is especially valuable, and may surprise
us a little in a mediæval writer. It is the
same thought which Robert Browning has
developed in *Rabbi Ben Ezra* :—

> "Let us not always say
> 'Spite of this flesh to-day
> I strove, made head, gained ground upon the whole!'
> As the bird wings and sings
> Let us cry, 'All good things
> Are ours, nor soul helps flesh more, now, than flesh helps
> soul!'"

From the morbid emotionalism which disfigures the writings of many mystics of the
cloister Julian is entirely free. She never
broods on the thought of Christ as the
Bridegroom of the individual soul, though
personal love and pity for the suffering
Redeemer are expressed in touching and
tender language. "How might any pain be
more to me than to see Him that is all my
life, all my bliss, and all my joy, suffer?"
When the thought came to her that she
ought rather to look up to heaven, to God
the Father, than to the Cross of Christ, she

"saw well, with the faith that she felt," that "there was nothing betwixt the Cross and heaven that might have harmed me," and she answered inwardly, with all the might of her soul, "Nay, I may not, for Thou art my heaven." "For I would liefer have been in pain till doomsday than to come to heaven otherwise than by Him." There are three ways in which, she tells us, we ought to think about the Passion of Christ: first, the hard pains which He suffered; second, the love that made Him suffer them; and third, the joy and bliss that made Him well satisfied to suffer them. In all this there is nothing overstrained or unwholesome—only the pure devotion of a healthy and loving nature. Our relations with Christ are thus described, with a charming echo of the language of knightly chivalry: "Our courteous Lord willeth that we should be as homely with Him as heart may think or soul may desire. But beware that we take not so recklessly this homeliness as to leave courtesy. For our Lord Himself is sovereign homeliness, and as homely as He is, so courteous He is; for He is very courteous. And the blessed creatures that shall be in heaven with Him without end, He will have them like to Himself in all things. And to be like our Lord perfectly, it is our very salvation and our full bliss."

We like to think of Julian's cell visited not only by grown-up people seeking consolation or advice, but by the little children of the neighbourhood. She loved children, as her Master loved them. "I understood no higher stature in this life than childhood," she says.

The end of this fragrant little book is in character with all the rest. The same faith and love, the same sunny confidence and hope, breathe through it. "When the doom is given, and we be all brought up above, then shall we clearly see in God the secret things which be now hid to us." "For charity pray we all." But God worketh in us; it is His will that we pray for, and it is by His grace that we pray. "Thus will our good Lord be prayed to, as by the understanding that I took of His own meaning, and of the sweet words where He saith full merrily: 'I am the Ground of thy beseeching.' For truly I saw and understood that He showed it for that He willeth to have it known more than it is; in which knowing He will give us grace to love Him and cleave to Him. For He beholdeth His heavenly treasure with so great love on earth that He willeth to give us more light and solace in heavenly joy, in drawing to Him of our hearts, for sorrow and darkness which we are in. From the time that it was showed I desired oftentimes to witten what was our Lord's meaning. And fifteen years after, and more, I was answered in ghostly understanding, saying thus: 'Wouldst thou learn thy Lord's meaning in this thing? Learn it well: Love was His meaning. Who showed it thee? Love. What showed He thee? Love. Wherefore showed it He? For Love. Hold thee therein and thou shalt learn and know more in the same. But thou shalt never know nor learn therein other thing without end.' Thus was I learned that Love was our Lord's meaning. And I saw full clearly that ere God made us He loved

us; which love was never slacked, nor ever
shall be. And in this love He hath done
all His works; and in this love He hath
made all things profitable to us; and in this
love our life is everlasting. In our making
we had beginning; but the love wherein He
made us was in Him from without beginning;
in which love we have our beginning. And
all this shall we see in God, without end."

So Julian lived for the rest of her long life
on the sweet memory of the one revelation
which came to her during her grievous sickness, and the meaning of which became fully
plain to her fifteen years later. There is a
very curious parallel in the biography of
Erskine of Linlathen, a Scottish layman of
great sanctity and beauty of character, who
lived within in the last century. Principal
Shairp recounts of him: "He spoke of the
awful silence of God, how it sometimes
became oppressive, and the heart longed to
hear, in answer to its cry, some audible
voice. And then he added: 'But it has not
always been silence to me. I have had one
revelation: it is now, I am sorry to say, a

matter of memory with me. It was not a revelation of anything that was new to me. After it, I did not know anything which I did not know before. But it was a joy for which one might bear any sorrow. I felt the power of love—that God is love, that He loved me, that He had spoken to me, and then, after a long pause, that He had broken silence to me.'"

LECTURE III

THE picture of human life as a spiritual Jacob's ladder, on which angels are for ever ascending and descending, and which we all have to climb step by step, is as old as the rule of St Benedict. The idea of a gradual ascent, not in time or place, but from stage to stage of reality, leaving behind us the vain shadows of earth, and beholding ever more clearly the mysteries of Divine truth, has always been dear to mystics. Charts of spiritual progress have been drawn up in large numbers, till in the later Romanist theology a kind of geography of the saint's journey has been constructed, not less fanciful than Bunyan's *Pilgrim's Progress*. But it is not a sign of Protestant prejudice to assert that the mystical literature of the pre-Reformation period is more valuable and edifying than anything that the Roman Church has produced since. Nor is it, I hope, a sign of insular prejudice to prefer the writings of old English divines to anything of the same kind produced on the Continent. For my own part, much as I admire the philosophical genius of Eckhart, the poetical fervour of Suso, and the robust eloquence of Tauler, I find in the *Scale of Perfection*, by Walter Hylton, Canon of Thurgarton, who died in 1396, teaching not less sound, not less winning, not less eloquent, than the best examples of the more celebrated German mystics. And so I have decided to devote one of my six lectures to a book which most of you, I dare say, have never even heard of. I cannot promise that there will be the same amount of personal interest as in Julian's *Revelations*. We have now to deal with a methodical treatise on the spiritual life, instead of with the record of a strange personal experience. Walter Hylton keeps his own individuality in the background. We can only guess that he was not a stranger to some of the Divine favours

L

which he describes. But the book has a charm of its own in the shrewd common-sense and flashes of humour which distinguish it from such scholastic treatises on mysticism as were written by Richard and Hugo of St Victor, Albertus Magnus, and Gerson. These latter are never likely to be disinterred except by a few scholars; the *Scale of Perfection* only needs to be known, in order to take high rank among the best specimens of devotional literature.

I shall give you a brief analysis of the book, omitting some sections, which are of less interest than the rest.

The first step on the ladder of contemplation is knowledge of the facts of religion, which, however, is only a shadow of true contemplation, because it may be had without love. It is like the water at Cana, which must be turned into wine by grace.

The second part consists of mere feeling, without light in the understanding. A man "cannot tell what it is, but he feeleth it is well, for it is a gift of God." This part has two degrees. The lower degree cometh and goeth as He willeth who giveth it; "whoso hath it, let him be humble, and thank God and keep it secret." The higher part is rest and quietness, "when all the Church's prayers and hymns and ministrations are turned, as it were, into spiritual mirth and sweet harmony."

The third part consists in a combination of knowledge with perfect love. It may begin in this life, but in its fulness it is reserved for heaven, and can only be enjoyed there. In this state is fulfilled what St Paul says to the Corinthians: "He that is joined unto the Lord is one Spirit," or as the same apostle says in his second epistle to the same church: "Whether we are beside ourselves, it is unto God; or whether we are of sober mind, it is unto you. For the love of Christ constraineth us." In this blessed state we are made like to our Lord, and are transformed into His likeness. "We all with unveiled face reflecting as a mirror the glory of the Lord, are transformed into the same image from glory to glory, even as from the Lord the Spirit." Hylton does not profess to have experienced this rapturous condition: he speaks of it on the authority of others. "As I gather from holy men, the time of it is very short; for he soon after returneth to a sobriety of bodily feeling." "The time is very short"; Hylton does not tell us how long it lasts, on an average. But there is a curious consensus among visionaries that the time occupied by a trance is "about half an hour." St Teresa is one of those who has named this duration. Hylton says that this is a special gift, not very common, and that, as we might expect, it is most fully enjoyed by those who lead a solitary life, devoted to religious exercises.

As for the strange physical and psychical phenomena which sometimes accompany this state—sights and sounds and odours, a sensation of burning heat in the breast, apparitions of various kinds—Hylton bids us " be wary." He does not doubt that such things really take place, but it is by no means easy to determine whether they are sent by God or are a snare of the devil. The best test is to ask ourselves whether they tend to distract our minds from our devotions and from good actions. If they do, they are delusions sent

by the Evil One, and should not be attended
to. Here we see traces of a difficulty which
has greatly exercised the minds of Roman
Catholic directors in later times. Roman
Catholic books on mysticism consist largely
of descriptions of "mystical phenomena," and
of cautions against being deceived by diabolical
counterfeits. Nearly all the saints who have
believed themselves to be the recipients of
these special favours have also been plagued
by the wiles of the devil, who is most active
and insidious in his attempts to trip up
the holiest characters. The criterion recom-
mended by the mystics is much the same as
in Hylton's advice. The vision, like other
things, must be known by its fruits. The
"mystical phenomena" described by Hylton
are much the same as those which appear in
the later history of mysticism—unaccountable
sights, sounds, or smells, apparitions, and a
strange feeling of burning heat in the breast.

The natural causes of these phenomena,
which cannot be due entirely to suggestion
and expectation, have not yet been fully ascer-
tained. We may almost say that the worth

of a mystical treatise varies inversely with
the importance which it attaches to these
experiences, which, of course, were formerly
ascribed to supernatural agencies. Hylton
gives them a very small place indeed.

The psychology of the Middle Ages was
not quite in accordance with modern mental
science.. Memory was often elevated to the
rank of a primary faculty, by the side of
will and feeling. But Hylton's scheme of
the faculties and their place in the spiritual
life bears a curious resemblance to that of
some recent Hegelians. Mr McTaggart, in
his *Studies in Hegelian Dialectic*, holds that
the will and the intellect are unharmonised
factors in our personality, which partially
contradict and thwart each other until they
find their reconciling principle in love. Love
is the supreme activity of the person, which
transcends the disharmony between the ethical
and the intellectual parts of our nature. So
Hylton says that a man may have virtues in
reason and will, without having the love of
them in the affection. " But when, by the
grace of Jesus, and by spiritual and bodily

exercises, *reason is turned into light, and will into love*, then hath he virtues in affection." Until these virtues are thus turned into affection, a man may have what Hylton calls the second degree of contemplation, but not the third and highest.

Of Prayer, he says that it is not the cause of grace, but the means by which it comes into the soul. Contemplatives should beware of the temptation to abandon vocal prayer for meditation. It is only those who are far advanced in the spiritual life who can safely allow the "prayer of quiet" to occupy the chief place in their devotions. When we meditate, the best subject on which to fix our thoughts is the humanity of Jesus Christ. Especially helpful are meditations on His Passion and death. We should remember how central this subject was in the teaching of St Paul. "We preach Christ crucified, unto Jews a stumbling-block, and unto Gentiles foolishness; but unto them that are called, both Jews and Greeks, Christ the Power of God and the Wisdom of God" (1 Cor. i. 23, 24). This passage shows the normal and proper course of meditation on the Second Person of the Trinity. We should begin by dwelling on the human Christ, and especially on His sufferings for our redemption. We should not allow the Jewish craving for miracles, nor the Greek craving for philosophy, to distract our minds from the Cross on Calvary. But our devotion is not to end in pity and affection for the human Sufferer. We must not be content till we can see in Him the legitimate satisfaction of what both Jews and Greeks really desire for their soul's peace. Christ is no magician, no wonder-worker, but He is the Power of God. Christ is no abstract metaphysical principle, no logical category, but He is the Wisdom of God.

"The plain highway to contemplation is for a man to enter into himself, that he may know his own soul, and the powers thereof." The result of such introspection is to reveal to us at the same time the greatness and the littleness of man—his high calling and his low estate. We see the great nobility and dignity of the soul, and the wretchedness and miseries into which we have brought it by our sins.

We are fallen creatures. We are not in possession of our birthright. How, then, are we to regain what of right belongs to us, and has been forfeited by us? "In one word— Jesus—thou hast all that thou hast lost." So speaks this truly evangelical Catholic. But "by the name of Jesus," he adds, "I mean all that the name betokens." He does not wish us to use the *name* as a spell to conjure with, but to find out what the name really means to us and all the world. The piece of money—the groat, as he calls it—is lost in thy house. That is to say, the Divine treasure lies hidden in thy soul. Jesus sleeps in thy ship, as He once slept in the little ship on the Lake of Gennesaret. "Wake Him!" But is it necessary to wake Him? "Hardly so," says Hylton. "Thou sleepest oftener to Him than He to thee." "As long as Jesus findeth not His image refound in thee, He is a stranger to thee and far from thee." Yes, it is not that the Christ in us is asleep. We are asleep, He is awake. We

M

are abroad, He is at home. He is always
ready; it is we who are unready. When we
desire to enter into ourselves, and search in
our hearts for the hid treasure, we should cease
for a time from bodily works and business,
and think of nothing outside. Then, when
our minds are fixed steadily on the unseen
realities—on God and our own souls—what
shall we see? Not the gracious figure of
Jesus, at first, but another image, a dark and
ill-favoured image, the likeness of our own
soul, which hath neither light of knowledge
nor feeling of love for God. "If you look
carefully," says Hylton to his reader, "you will
see it all wrapped up and tied and bound
with black and foul bands of sin." This is
what St Paul calls the "body of sin"
(Rom. vi. 6), and the "body of death." This
dark shadow, the body of sin and death, you
bear about with you always. What is it
like? It is like no bodily thing; for *it is no
real thing*, as you will find at last if you
follow my admonitions. It is not a real
thing; it is nought else but darkness of
conscience, and lack of light and love. If

your soul were reformed, according to the image of Jesus, you would no longer find this ugly and negative shape, this nothingness made visible, but Jesus. Until this blessed change has happened in you, you find within yourself only emptiness, darkness, and heaviness. It is no wonder, then, that introspection seems to you irksome and depressing. "It seems a hundred years till you are out of yourself, in quest of some bodily delight or vain thought. He that cometh home and findeth nought there but dirt and smoke and a scolding wife, will quickly run out of it." "But do not you run out of it," says Hylton. "Stay at home, and endure the pains and the discomfort. For behind this nothingness, behind this dark and formless shape of evil, is Jesus hid in His joy."

The dark image, as I have said, is nothing. But how, then, can it be an image? It is a false inordinate love of thyself. The body of sin and death is self-love or selfishness. Out of it come the seven deadly sins, flowing in seven channels. Thus regarded, it is not altogether nothing, but much that is bad.

But perhaps you will say, "I have dedicated myself to God. I have forsaken the world and its temptations — I have no worldly business, no carnal pleasures. How, then, can this image be so strong in me?" "Alas!" says Hylton, "thou art like a man who had in his garden a foul cistern with many outlets; and he went and stopped up the outlets, and thought that all was well." To retire from the world is only to stop the outlets of temptation. Beware of the spring within thee. If this is foul, its pollution will force its way out somehow. I will tell you how to stop up this spring. Pride is the principal river. If love and praise and other favours from men be dear to thy heart, and if thou turn them into vain gladness and make them, as it were, thy payment and thy due, thinking seriously in thy heart that men ought to praise thy life, and attend to thy words more than to those of other men; and if, on the contrary, when men reprove thee and set thee at nought, hold thee for a fool or a hypocrite, slander thee or speak evil of thee falsely, or in any other way annoy thee

unreasonably, thou feelest in thy heart a great
malice and rising in thy heart against them,
with unwillingness to suffer any shame or
disgrace in the eyes of the world; if it be
thus with thee, it is a token that there is
much pride in that dark image of thine.

Now turn the dark image, the body of sin
and death, upside down, and look well into
it. There are two limbs, of anger and envy,
fastened to it, which hinder charity. From
them come a variety of evil things, hatred,
suspicion, unkindness, evil speaking, and the
like. Among the fruits of anger and envy
he names one fault which prevents his
injunctions under this head from being
commonplace. We are to beware of "a
harshness and bitterness to all sinful men, and
others who will not do as we think they
should, with a great desire and eagerness,
under cover of charity and justice, that they
should be well punished and chastised for
their sins." This touches upon a very
common weakness of good people, from
which few of us, probably, are entirely free.
Most of us have a favourite aversion among

the vices, and take small shame to ourselves
for the glee with which we hear of trans-
gressors being "well punished and chastised."
Aristotle regards it as a moral duty to
rejoice at the misfortunes of the bad, and to
grieve over the prosperity of the wicked. To
sympathise whole - heartedly with right and
justice, and to rejoice in every triumph of
the good cause over the bad, without loss of
Christian charity, is one of the most difficult
moral tasks. "Thou shouldest love the man,
be he ever so sinful," says Hylton, "and
hate the sin in every man, whatever he be."
Then follows a sentence which reminds us of
Eckhart's contemptuous reference to the dead
bones of saints, which "can neither give nor
take anything." "There is no great excellence
in watching and fasting till thy head aches,
nor in running to Rome or Jerusalem with
bare feet, nor in building churches and
hospitals." But it is a great sign of
excellence if a man can love a sinner
while yet hating the sin. Did not our
Lord show love to Judas, though He knew
of his covetousness and peculations in the

present, and of his treason in the near future?

Covetousness is the next vice that we observe in the dark image of sin. It is easier to forsake worldly goods than the love of them. "Perhaps thou hast not forsaken thy covetousness, but only changed the object of it. Formerly it was a silver dish, now it is a copper. A foolish change, which shows thee to be no clever merchant!" Consider instead whether you would mind losing what you have, or whether you would be angry with him who took it. St Augustine says beautifully: "Too little doth he love Thee, O God, who loveth anything with Thee which he loves not for Thee." (From Augustine, *Confessions* x. 29.) "But God knows," says Hylton, "that I am teaching far more than I practise." This humble parenthesis is characteristic of our author, and is very appropriate after he has quoted so terribly exacting a demand as that of St Augustine's words. "But," he goes on in a graceful sentence, "it would be a comfort to my heart, if, though I have not this virtue myself, I should have it in thee."

To deal with the sin of Gluttony is difficult, says Hylton, because it is rooted in natural necessity. "Slay unreasonable delights and voluntary sensual pleasures. If you have given way to any indulgence which comes under this head, pray for forgiveness, and then set about some other business; but think no further of thy frailty, for it is not worth such attention, and you will not destroy it in this way." This advice, indeed, may be applied to most kinds of temptation. "When thou attackest the root of sin, fix thy thoughts more upon the God whom thou desirest than upon the sin which thou abhorrest."

In concluding Book I. of the first part of his treatise, Hylton reminds us that parts of it pertain only to one in the contemplative (as opposed to the active) state of life. I have chosen the precepts which are of most general application; but in truth there is not much of the *Scale of Perfection* which applies *only* to monks.

In Book II. he returns to the "image of

sin" which is disclosed to our introspective
eye. The reformation of it must take place
partly in this life and partly in the future
life. As regards the present life, the reformation may be in faith, or in feeling. The
former suffices for salvation, the latter earns
a surpassing great reward, and may be had
only through great spiritual pains. By the
first, the "image of sin" is not destroyed,
but is left intact in point of feeling. (That
is, the commission of sin would still give
pleasure, though it is avoided from a sense
of duty.) The second puts out the pleasure
felt in sin.

The paragraphs on the sacraments, which
follow, are somewhat disappointing. There
is more of superstitious, non-ethical, *magical*
doctrine, especially in dealing with the
Eucharist, than we should have expected in
so enlightened and independent a thinker.

The soul that is "reformed in feeling," to
adopt Hylton's phrase, must remember that
such a state "lasteth not always." We must
not expect to be delivered from the life and
death struggle between the law in our

members and law of our mind. St Paul
himself was torn and tormented by this
conflict; and if St Paul so suffered, how can
any of us hope to escape? The strife must
needs be; for our nature is the battle-ground
of good and evil forces. "Fair is a man's
soul, and foul is a man's soul; foul without,
like a beast; and fair within, like an angel."
Like the bride in the Canticles, the soul is
"black, but comely." The pure brightness
of the Divine image is encrusted with a foul
covering of sin.

Some will say : " I would fain love God and
be good if I could, but I have not the grace
for it; and so I hope I shall be excused."
To such I answer: "True it is, as you say,
that you have not grace, and that therefore
you cannot be good. But it is your own
fault that you have not grace. Men unfit
themselves for receiving grace, and therefore
do not receive it, in various ways. Some are
froward, and think their sins so sweet that
they will not part with them. They cannot
bring themselves to submit to penance and
mortification, and so they remain bound in

their chains. Others begin to dispose themselves for grace, but their will is weak.
They condemn temptation when it comes,
but do not put it from them, and end by
assenting to it. There are also some who
are so blind and brutish as to say that there
is no other life besides this. Their maxim
is, 'Let us eat and drink, for to-morrow we
die.' Of such no more need be said."

Part II. of the *Scale of Perfection* deals
with the higher rungs of the spiritual ladder.
Again, he insists that without pains and
industry none can attain to what he calls
reformation in feeling as well as in faith. A
man can no more make a sudden ascent from
the lowest to the highest than he can climb
from the bottom to the top of a ladder at
one step.

Why do so few attain to the higher stage
of perfection? Many are satisfied if they
can save their souls, and reach even the
lowest degree in heaven. It is dangerous to
aim at what is barely sufficient, as we may
just miss it; but in busy people who are
living in the world such want of spiritual

ambition is excusable. But it is perilous for
a soul which feels itself to have arrived at
the lower stage of "reformation in faith" to
rest there, and be content to climb no further.
For there is no standing still in the spiritual
life : if we are not going on, we must be
going back. So Augustine says : "Say but,
It is sufficient, and you are lost. Ever
increase, ever march on, ever advance"
(*Serm.* 169). If a man has been drawn up
out of a pit, will he refuse to go any further
than the brink? Will he remain where one
step must plunge him again into the depths?
And how can a man have enough of God's
grace? Grace is, no doubt, the free gift of
God, but it is usually not given without the
fullest co-operation on the part of the soul.
True humility is a great help here. "Humility
saith, 'I am nothing, I have nothing, I desire
nothing, but Jesus.' This makes good music
in the soul. Compared with Jesus, who is
all, thou art nothing." The love of Jesus
is thus the foundation of true humility.

And what are the enemies? Chiefly, carnal
desires and vain fears. But hold thou on thy

way, desiring nothing at all except the love of
the Lord Jesus. When thou art tempted,
answer the tempter alway on this wise: "I
am nothing, I have nothing, I desire nothing,
save the love of Jesus only." Do not ransack
thy memory to confess again what is past and
gone. Hold on thy way, and think only of
Jerusalem, the goal of thy journey. The
tempting spirits will try to discourage thee.
They will whisper in thine ear: "Thou canst
never fulfil all these resolutions. Return to
thine old life and do as others do." Then
thou must answer them: "Since I was created
to love God, I will ever desire and hope
for it, even though I should never arrive at
it." When discouragement has failed to shake
thy resolution, they will try other methods.
They will bring it about that all thy good
shall be evil-spoken of, and that whatsoever
thou doest shall be taken ill. In this way
thy tempters will endeavour to stir thee up to
anger or to melancholy, or to ill-will against
thy neighbours. But do thou use this remedy.
Take the Lord Jesus into thy mind, and
trouble not thyself. Think of thy lesson—

that thou art nothing, that thou hast nothing, and desirest nothing, save Jesus only. Do not dwell in thought on thy sins and defects, for fear of thine enemies. These enemies, when they have failed to achieve their purpose in this attempt also, will next try the effect of flattery. They will tell thee, and try to persuade thee, that all men praise and love and honour thee. They will not move thee; for thou wilt reject all such suggestions, esteeming them to be mere stratagems of the enemy, as indeed they are, venom sweetened with honey. Refuse it and have none of it, and say that thy wish is to be with Jesus.

All these hindrances and temptations will beset thee. And yet, so long as a man suffers his thoughts to run at large, as it were, about the world, to wander unchecked whithersoever they choose to roam, he perceives few of these hindrances. But as soon as he withdraws his thoughts and desires from worldly things, and fixes them on one thing only—the love of Jesus—then he will feel many painful hindrances. It is not a sign

that all is well with us if we feel no hindrances.
We ought to feel many.

This desire which fills thy heart is verily
Jesus. It is He who worketh it in thee;
it is He who giveth it thee. He desireth
in thee, and He is desired. He is all, and
doth all. Thou art only an instrument in
His hands. "O send out Thy light and
Thy truth, that they may lead me, and bring
me to Thy holy hill, and to Thy dwelling."

The necessity of concentration, and the
danger of indulging freely in discursive thought
which dissipates our energies and distracts
our attention, are topics which we encounter
very frequently in the mystics. They are
fond of using the metaphor of "darkness"
for the state in which the mind is a *tabula
rasa*, ready for any purely spiritual impression
to act upon it. Hylton also uses this expression. The "good darkness," he says, is when
the soul through grace is so free, so gathered
up into itself, that it is not distracted by any
earthly thing. "This is a rich nothing, when
the soul is at rest as to earthly thoughts, but
very busy in thinking of Jesus." "It is not

all darkness or nothing, when the soul thinketh thus." "For Jesus, who is both love and light, is in this darkness, whether it be painful or restful." If thou wouldest know whether thou art in this secure darkness or not, ask whether thou covetest anything in this life for itself alone. Ask this question of each of thy five senses. If they make answer to thee honestly, "I would see nothing, hear nothing, taste and touch nothing, but would have my affections wholly fixed on God," then thou art in this profitable darkness. Although "this lasteth, whole and entire, but for a short time," accustom thyself to dwell in this profitable darkness, for little by little the light of spiritual knowledge will arise in thee. Then thou wilt experience the truth of those words of the prophet Isaiah: "The people that walked in darkness have seen a great light, and they who walked in darkness and in the shadow of death, upon them hath the light shined." Thou art not yet at Jerusalem, the end of thy journey; "but by some small flashes of light, which shine through the chinks of the city walls, thou

wilt be able to see it long before thou comest
to it."

In these paragraphs Hylton has been using
the common language of the mystics. The
"Divine darkness" is a familiar idea in
Christian mysticism from Dionysius downwards.
Equally familiar is the warning which follows
—against the "false light." Readers of the
Theologia Germanica will remember how
earnestly we are warned against the danger
of mistaking some devil-sent *ignis fatuus* for
the true light of the Divine Presence. This
is how Hylton deals with it: "But now
beware of the mid-day fiend, that feigneth
light as if it came from Jerusalem, but does
not so." How shall we distinguish between
the true and the false light? Sometimes we
see a light shining between two black rainy
clouds, a light which looks like the sun, but
is not. So it is in spiritual things. There
are some men who, as far as externals go,
have forsaken the pomps and vanities of the
world, and have renounced all the deadly
sins, but who give no industry to examining
themselves and purging their hearts. Then,

O

because they have made this external renunciation, they fancy themselves to be already
holy, and "presently begin to preach, and
teach other men, as if they had received the
grace of understanding, to preach truth and
righteousness to their neighbours." But their
light comes from the mid-day fiend, as they
will see if they look carefully. For it shines
between two black rainy clouds, of which
the upper is presumption and self-exaltation,
and the lower undervaluing our neighbour.
If these feelings are present, though the
knowledge itself be true, "it is from the
fiend if it comes all of a sudden, or from a
man's own wit if it comes by study." Men
of this kind are full of pride, and see it not;
and all their preaching tends to strife and
discord, and reproof of divers states and
persons. "But where envying and strife is,
there is confusion and every evil work"
(James iii. 16). The true sun only shines in
a clear sky. The "good darkness" is marked
by humility and charity; "and I believe," says
Hylton, "that after true darkness has gone
before, the false light never comes."

This, then, is to be our safeguard, if we
wish to be led by the Spirit, instead of
submitting ourselves to human guidance. We
shall be led aright, and need not fear to be
misled by the Evil One, if we are in humility
and charity. They are also tests whether
the light that is in us is in truth light, or
something worse than darkness. If we are
proud or uncharitable, we have not the Spirit of
God, and should be far safer in leading-strings,
obeying and following external authority.

But is it necessary to pass through the
"good darkness" at all? Is it necessary for
us to abstract our minds from external things,
as the mystics of the cloister seem always
to recommend? We are not here concerned
with the follies of the hesychasts and quietists,
or with the death in life of the Indian *yogi*.
Such a life is a mere *reductio ad absurdum*
of the philosophy on which it is based. But
is not the advice of the cloister-mystics infected
by the same fallacy—that we can reach the
infinite by mere negation of the finite, stripping
ourselves bare of all that belongs to our
terrestrial existence in the hope of anticipating

the life which will be ours when we have passed beyond the bourne of time and space? Is it not all part of that philosophy of dreams which teaches, with Shelley, that—

"Life, like a dome of many-coloured glass,
    Stains the white radiance of eternity"?

I have said, in my introductory Lecture, that the temptation in mysticism is to grasp at immediate apprehension of Divine truth before the time. The error is not in believing that a real knowledge of and communion with God is possible to men, but in supposing that it is given to start with. The strength of the best mystical teaching lies just in the recognition that we must "die to live" in every part of our spiritual nature. Our earthly affections, our appreciation of natural beauty, our intellectual speculations, must all be baptized into Christ's death. They must pass through a transformation, they must be lost and found again. There must be an apparent loss, as part of the real gain. So long as this mysterious law of our being — death everywhere the gate of life—is remembered, mystical theology is sane and sound; when it is for-

gotten, dangerous tendencies always manifest
themselves. This is the truth which underlies the doctrine of the negative road, and of
the Divine darkness. The perversions of it
are partly due to the strange psychological
experience of the blank trance, a kind of
self-hypnotisation in which the mind sometimes
receives indelible impressions.

Violent emotional fervours, says Hylton, to
whom I now return after a brief digression, do
not belong to a high state, but are rather
characteristic of beginners, "who for the
littleness and weakness of their souls cannot
bear the smallest touch of God." This is
quite in accordance with what other authorities
tell us ; though they more often suggest that
these rapturous joys are given by God as an
encouragement to those who are just beginning
to advance on the way of holiness.

A soul that would know spiritual things
must first know itself. If we do not know
ourselves, we cannot know anything above
ourselves. Do not look for your soul inside
your body, or you will never find it. The
soul is not inside or outside your body. It is

no bodily thing, with a spatial existence, but an invisible life. It would be truer to say that the body is in the soul, than that the soul is in the body. "Consider thy soul as a life, immortal and invisible, which has in itself the power to know the sovereign truth, and love the sovereign goodness, which is God. When thou feelest this, thou wilt feel something of thy true self. Seek thyself in no other place. The more fully and worthily thou thinkest of the nature and worthiness of a reasonable soul, the better thou wilt see into thyself. Do not form any image of a bodily shape, when thou thinkest about thy soul." This caution is also valuable. Half-unconsciously we do often think of our souls as a kind of ghosts, shadowy creatures like phantasms of living men. It is worth while to remind ourselves that the soul, as soul, has nothing to do with the categories of space and time.

The soul must first know itself. But it must not rest in self-knowledge. For the soul is but a mirror in which to behold God. The soul is a mirror. Therefore the first requisite is that it should be kept bright and clean, and the second is that it should be held well up from the earth.

Hylton then proceeds to speak of the love of God. He says that there are three kinds, or degrees, in the love of man to God. The first is for faith only, without any devout imagination or spiritual knowledge. The second works upon us through the imagination of Jesus in His sacred humanity. The third comes through spiritual sight of the Godhead in the sacred humanity. This classification is worth quoting, because it shows that Hylton does not contemplate the possibility of the human Christ ever becoming unnecessary to us. The criticism has often been passed upon the Platonising theologians of the third century, Clement of Alexandria and Origen, that the "Gnostic," or perfect Christian in their system, needs Christ only as the Logos, and no longer as the Incarnate Son, Jesus. But Hylton, like Julian of Norwich in my last Lecture, knows that we can never get beyond the human Christ. "Thou art my heaven," says Julian; and Hylton will be more than content if he can dwell with loving and clear sight upon the Godhead in the sacred humanity. Spiritual love that comes through the understanding is better than that which comes only through the imagination. All bodily beholdings are but means by which the soul is led to this. The words of our Lord to Mary Magdalene, "Touch me not," may be interpreted to mean, "Worship me in thine understanding." The outward manifestations of Divine favour, which in the later Roman Catholic mysticism play such a dominant part under the name of mystical phenomena, are for Hylton only tokens of inward grace, like the cloven tongues on the day of Pentecost, which were a purely external sign.

In Part III. Hylton begins by saying: "I would not by these discourses limit God's working by the law of my speaking. I do not wish to imply that God worketh so in a soul and no otherwise. No, I meant not so. I hope well also that He worketh otherwise, in ways which pass my wit and feeling."

The soul has two kinds of feelings: one external, through the five bodily senses, and one internal, through the spiritual senses or faculties of the soul. The spiritual senses or faculties Hylton considers to be four in number: wit, memory, understanding, and will. "When these faculties are through grace perfect in all understanding and spiritual wisdom, then the soul hath new feelings which are the offspring of grace." When St Paul bids the Ephesians to "be renewed in the spirit of your minds," he means " in the higher part of your reason." "Understanding is the mistress, imagination is the maid." Understanding is strong meat for men, imagination is milk for babes. Whatever psychologists may think of Hylton's analysis of human faculties, it is plain that he is mainly concerned in exalting the inward as compared with the outward, and disparaging those sensible images which often float before the mental vision of the contemplative, and which he is frequently tempted to overvalue.

We speak sometimes of "heaven opening to the eye of the soul." This, again, is a mere metaphor, which we must beware of taking literally. It is not the heaven above the

P

firmament, the depths of space above our heads, which opens to the eye of the soul. "The higher the soul soareth above the sun to see Jesus as God, the lower it falls, by reason of such an imagination." Nevertheless, this kind of sight is tolerable in simple souls who have no better way of seeing Him who is invisible. Hylton here seems to go beyond Benjamin Whichcote's "Heaven is first a temper, and then a place," and to repudiate the idea of a local heaven altogether. But he would probably admit that for almost all persons, and not for "simple souls" alone, it is helpful and almost necessary to envisage the eternal world under the forms of space as well as of time. The natural impulse which bids us to "lift up our eyes," as well as our hearts, when we pray to God or praise Him, need not be resisted, though it is well to remember sometimes that God is here as much as anywhere else, and that we need not send our prayers on a long journey to find Him. "Spiritual things," says Plotinus, "are separated from each other only by difference and antagonism of nature, not by place."

"What is heaven to a reasonable soul?
Verily nought else but Jesus God." A striking
sentence, which again reminds us of Hylton's
contemporary Julian. God alone is above the
nature of the soul; whosoever seeth God seeth
heaven. The soul is above every bodily thing;
no idea of local elevation should be entertained,
as if we needed to be transported to some other
part of space in order to come near to God.
Similarly, we must be careful to remember
that "within" is a mere metaphor when used
of spiritual things. It is commonly said that
the soul should see God "within" all things,
and "within" itself. We may use these
expressions, but they are metaphors. God is
not within the soul as a kernel is within a nut,
or as a lesser bodily thing is within a greater.

Other expressions which we use about God
are equally metaphorical, *e.g.*, "God is Light."
God is compared to light, because He is the
Truth; and He is compared to a consuming
fire, because He cleanses the soul like fire.
But let us not think much of fire the element,
in connection with God. We must try to look
not on the things that are seen, which are

temporal, but on the things that are not seen, which are eternal. And eternity is the knowledge, or rather the knowing, of God, and of Jesus Christ whom He sent.

What is the relation between the beatific vision and the fruition of Divine love? The full bliss of the soul, says Hylton, is the love that proceeds from sight. " Love proceeds from knowledge, and not knowledge from love." The more God is known, the more He is loved. Here some might object that the best way to get to know a person is to love him, and that those who reserve their affection till their companion's character is fully explored, will never either know nor love him. And in the case of love to God felt by man, since our knowledge must always be so small, love must come first, and knowledge follow as its reward. But our author is here speaking of the perfect love that casteth out fear. This can only be the result of knowledge. The assertion that love is the final crown, higher than knowledge, is necessary as a safeguard against intellectualism. We must not turn religion into

philosophy. Hylton is here quite in agree-
ment with the Christian Platonists, including
Clement of Alexandria. They give knowledge
a very high place, but not the highest.

"When God crowns our merits," says St
Augustine, "He crowns only His own gifts."
This maxim is thoroughly in accordance with
Hylton's teaching. The greatest boon that
God ever gives is the gift of Himself. First
He gives us the lower love, which keeps us
from sinning. Then he opens the eye of
the soul, that it may see the Divinity of
Jesus Christ, and adore His nature. Love
is master of the soul when it makes the soul
forget herself.

God gives us Himself. What does this
mean? The gift of Himself, the gift of the
Holy Ghost, is the gift of love. We should
ask of God nothing except the gift of love,
which is the Holy Ghost. There is no gift
of God which is both the giver and the gift,
except this of love. This alone saveth from
hell, and maketh the soul God's child and a
receiver of the heavenly heritage. This love
slayeth all the strivings of pride, and makes

the soul lose all relish for worldly honours. It slays "easily" all the stirrings of wrath and envy. Love alone can do this. "He who loves can more easily forget the wrong done to him than another man can forgive it." The true lover forgets rather than forgives, for there is no pride or contempt mixed with his forgiveness. Love also slays the other deadly sins. Covetousness, impurity, and gluttony cannot live in the soul where love reigns. Love sets all perishable things at one price, and values a precious stone no more than a piece of chalk.

What graces are those that the soul receiveth through love! I cannot speak of them, for they are more than I am able to express; but Love asketh and biddeth that I try to do so, and I hope that Love shall teach me. In the writings of holy men we find various things spoken of as the fruit of heavenly love—purity of spirit, rest, stillness, peace, burning affection, bright light—and there are many other words that they use. These graces are diverse in speech, but one in meaning. He that hath one hath all. It

is called *rest* by many holy men. It is called
rest, not because it makes us idle, but because
it makes the soul work gladly and softly. "It
is a most busy rest." Hylton here anticipates
the beautiful and helpful definition of rest as
"unimpeded activity." We are at rest when
what we do is no exertion to us; when it
makes us happy to do it; when there is
nothing within or without us that pulls us
back and tries to stop us from doing it. So
the Sabbath-rest of God, and of the Divine
Word of God, is described in the verse,
"My Father worketh hitherto, and I work."

But we must expect checks and disappoint-
ments in our ascent of the ladder of perfection.
Sometimes the grace to behold Jesus is for
a time withdrawn. Then we are painfully
conscious of our own miserable existence, and
we are assailed by carnal hopes and fears.
Not that we are left altogether to ourselves
in these states. It is the special, and not
the common grace, which is then withdrawn
from us. Common grace remains to us entire.
It is never withdrawn so long as a man's
heart is right with God,

Spiritual prayer does not consist of long petitions. The prayer of the contemplative is made up but of *one word*, says Hylton: as it is formed in the heart, so it sounds in the mouth. Both that which forms and that which utters it are the same thing; for the soul is by grace made whole and one in itself. The soul then asks not how it shall pray, for its eye is turned inwards to Jesus. These directions about prayer are not quite so clear as is Hylton's wont. But the most intimate prayer is in truth an experience that baffles description. It "consists of one word," or rather of no words; for words were invented to communicate our ideas to others; but where the barrier between persons is broken down by love and devotion, words become as unnecessary as they are inadequate.

When we feel our souls stirred by grace, says Hylton, we need not be afraid of being deceived. "Trust thy feeling fully when it is spiritual: keep it tenderly, and have great delicacy, not toward thyself, but it"; then grace itself will go on teaching thee.

"Jesus sometimes shows Himself as an

awful master, sometimes as a reverend teacher,
and sometimes as a loving spouse." The
spiritual things, shown by Jesus to the soul,
may be said to consist of all the truths contained in Holy Scripture. But there are
other truths also, which are not contained in
Holy Scripture, but which Jesus shows to some
of them that love Him. Such high truths,
which are at times made clear by inward
revelation, are the nature of all rational souls,
of the angels, and of the Trinity. "Love
and light go together in a pure soul."

Hylton is conscious that these last sections
of his book are somewhat inconsecutive, and
that they give an impression of superficial
treatment. "I touch on these things lightly,"
he says, "for the soul may *see* more in an hour
than can be written in the longest book."
With these words we leave him. They are
words which we should always remember
when we read devotional literature. We
should read such books on our knees, as it
were, for otherwise we cannot understand or
profit by them. Unless we bring a great
deal ourselves, we shall not get much from

Q

them. *Cor ad cor loquitur;* the hearts of
the writer and reader must beat together, or
the attempts of the saint to express what
cannot be said in words will seem only dark
and tiresome.

I have given two lectures to these
mediæval mystics of the cloister, with some
doubt as to how far I should be able to enlist
your sympathies with their type of piety. I
have chosen exceptionally favourable specimens
of monkish Christianity; but perhaps after
all you will say: These were lonely men and
women, and theirs is a lonely religion. "What
dost thou desire to know?" asks St Augustine
of himself. "God and thine own soul.
Nothing else? Nothing else at all." But
we moderns desire to know some other things
besides God and our own souls. We desire
to know the souls of other men, and the soul,
if it may be, of the external world, the soul
of nature. The difference between the two
views of life may be realised by comparing a
maxim which the saints of the cloister are
rather fond of quoting from Seneca: "Whenever I have been with other men, I return

less of a man than I was before," with the words of a typical nineteenth-century writer (Sir John Seeley) : " Solitude is the death of all but the strongest virtue." Rudyard Kipling thinks both are right :—

> " Down to Gehenna, or up to the throne,
> He travels the fastest who travels alone."

But the cloistered mystics are best regarded as specialists, who have sacrificed breadth for intensity. In my last three lectures I shall deal with developments of mysticism with which more persons now will sympathise : with that powerful and independent eighteenth-century thinker, William Law, Non - juror, moralist, and mystic ; with the religious poetry of nature, which will always have its classical example in Wordsworth ; and with the mystical conception of human life and human love, which is the inspiration and main theme of Robert Browning's poetry.

LECTURE IV

WILLIAM LAW

PROBABLY no period of English history has been so antagonistic to all that the word mysticism stands for, as the Georgian era. "Enthusiasm" was the bugbear of the eighteenth century. The word was used as a deadly controversial missile. A Georgian bishop is praised on his tombstone, which adorns, or rather disfigures, the walls of his cathedral, for his zeal, in repressing "enthusiasm." William Law, who is to be the subject of this lecture, lived in the eighteenth century, and was not ashamed to be an enthusiast. This alone would stamp him as a man of strong originality, and therefore an interesting personality. But he was, in fact, something more than this—a man of great intellectual power, of unusual

force of character, and the master of a
striking and attractive English style. He is
perhaps the foremost of our mystical divines.
I will give you first a short account of his
life, and will then discuss his writings and
their permanent value.

William Law was born in 1686, at the
village of King's Cliffe, in Northamptonshire.
His father was a tradesman of good standing,
and he was brought up in a religious home.
The *Rules for my Future Conduct,* which
he drew up, it would seem, about the time
when he went to Cambridge, remind us of the
austere conscientiousness which characterises
the *Serious Call.* They are worth quoting:

"I. To fix it deep in my mind that I have but one
business upon my hands—to seek for eternal happiness by
doing the will of God.

"II. To examine everything that relates to me in this
view, as it serves or obstructs this only end of life.

"III. To think nothing great or desirable because the
world thinks it so, but to form all my judgments of things
from the infallible Word of God, and direct my life according to it.

"IV. To avoid all concerns with the world, or the ways
of it, except where religion requires.

"V. To remember frequently, and impress it upon my
mind deeply, that no condition of this life is for enjoyment,

but for trial; and that every power, ability, or advantage we have, are all so many talents to be accounted for to the Judge of all the world.

"VI. That the greatness of human nature consists in nothing else but in imitating the divine nature. That therefore all the greatness of this world, which is not in good actions, is perfectly beside the point.

"VII. To remember often and seriously how much of time is inevitably thrown away, from which I can expect nothing but the charge of guilt; and how little there may be to come, on which an eternity depends.

"VIII. To avoid all excess in eating and drinking.

"IX. To spend as little time as I possibly can among such persons as can receive no benefit from me nor I from them.

"X. To be always fearful of letting my time slip away without some fruit.

"XI. To avoid all idleness.

"XII. To call to mind the presence of God whenever I find myself under any temptation to sin, and to have immediate recourse to prayer.

"XIII. To think humbly of myself, and with great charity of all others.

"XIV. To forbear from all evil speaking.

"XV. To think often of the life of Christ, and propose it as a pattern for myself.

"XVI. To pray privately thrice a day, besides my morning and evening prayers.

"XVII. To keep from [a blank space] as much as I can without offence.

"XVIII. To spend some time in giving an account of the day, previous to evening prayer. How have I spent the day? What sin have I committed? What temptations have I withstood? Have I performed all my duty?"

Not a bad set of rules for a young man at
the outset of his university life.   Law was
made a Fellow of Emmanuel in 1711, and
was ordained deacon in the same year.
Besides the ordinary studies, he had already
begun to study mysticism, in the writings of
Malebranche, a seventeenth-century theologian,
whose cardinal doctrine is that "We see all
things in God," the opposite, it will be
observed, of the equally mystical doctrine
that we see God in all things.   Malebranche's
doctrine, if held exclusively, leads logically
to the pan-nihilism of Indian philosophy ;
while the other side, if unduly emphasised,
tends to sentimental and non-ethical pantheism.

A man of Law's tastes might have been
happy as a resident Fellow at Cambridge.
But his rather obstinate conscientiousness led
him to become one of the Non-jurors, on the
accession of George I.   He announces his
intention of sacrificing his fellowship to his
scruples in a very manly letter addressed to
his brother.   "The multitude of swearers,"
he says, "has no influence upon me : their
reasons are only to be considered ; and every

one knows no good ones can be given for people swearing the direct contrary to what they believe. . . . I think I have consulted my best interest by what I have done; and I hope, upon second thoughts, you will think so too. I have hitherto enjoyed a large share of happiness; and if the time to come be not so pleasant, the memory of what is past shall make me thankful."

It is not certain where Law resided, or what he did, during the next ten years. The reports of his having held clerical offices are difficult to reconcile with his refusal to take the oaths, and are not made more probable by the absurd gossip, emanating from the same sources, that Law was "a gay parson, a great beau, and very sweet on the ladies." In 1717 he wrote his *Three Letters to the Bishop of Bangor* (Hoadly), in answer to that prelate's very anti-Catholic views of the Church; an exceedingly vigorous and telling attack, which raised its author to the front rank of controversialists. "You have left us," he tells the Bishop, "neither priests, nor sacraments, nor church; and what has your

Lordship given us in the room of all these advantages? Why, only sincerity. This is the great universal atonement for all; this is that which, according to your Lordship, will help us to the communion of saints hereafter, though we are in communion with anybody or nobody here." Six years later Law published a scathing denunciation of Mandeville's *Fable of the Bees; or Private Vices, Public Benefits.* Mandeville's essay was a clever and cynical defence of licence and selfishness. "I believe man, besides skin, flesh, bones, etc., that are obvious to the eye, to be a compound of various passions, which govern him by turns, whether he will or no." Law replies: "The definition is too general, because it seems to suit a wolf or a bear as exactly as yourself or a Grecian philosopher. . . . If you would prove yourself to be no more than a brute or an animal, how much of your life you need alter I cannot tell; but at least you must forbear writing against virtue, for no mere animal ever hated it." Law is not content with rebutting his opponent's theory of the origin of morality.

R

He gives his own. "In one sense, virtue had no origin—that is, there was never a time when it began to be—but it was as much without beginning as truth and goodness, which are in their natures as eternal as God. But moral virtue, if considered as the object of man's knowledge, began with the first man, and was as natural to him as it was natural to man to think and perceive or feel the difference between pleasure and pain. The reasonableness and fitness of actions themselves is a law to rational beings, nay, it is a law to which even the Divine nature is subject, for God is necessarily good and just, from the excellence of justice and goodness; and it is the will of God that makes moral virtue our law, and obliges us to act reasonably. Here, Sir, is the noble and divine origin of moral virtue. It is founded in the immutable relations of things, in the perfection and attributes of God, not in the pride of man or the craft of cunning politicians. Away, then, with your idle and profane fancies about the origin of moral virtue! For once, turn your eyes to heaven, and dare but own

a just and good God, and then you have
owned the true origin of religion and moral
virtue." The transition from sarcasm to noble
exhortation is characteristic of all Law's
controversial writing.

But his first important contribution to
positive theology was *A Practical Treatise
upon Christian Perfection*, which he defines
as "the right performance of our necessary
duties." Of this austere but beautiful treatise
I will say more when Law's theology is
under discussion.

In 1727 Law became tutor to Edward
Gibbon, father of the great historian, and
accompanied his pupil to Cambridge. He
also spent much time in the elder Gibbon's
house at Putney, where he became a centre
of an admiring circle, consisting of John
Byrom, a Fellow of Trinity, Cambridge, and
a sorry versifier; John and Charles Wesley,
his friendship with whom was destined to
be broken by a quarrel; Miss Hester Gibbon,
the daughter of the house; Mr Archibald
Hutcheson, M.P. for Hastings, who on his
death-bed advised his wife to make Law her

guide and counsellor in religious matters;
and two or three others of less importance.
Law, it must be confessed, made and kept
friends most easily when they were his
intellectual inferiors: there was something
stiff and uncompromising about him which
alienated some who might have met him on
equal terms. As long as John Wesley was
willing to consult him and follow his advice,
all went well. It was in answer to some
question of Wesley that Law replied in the
memorable words : " You would have a philosophical religion ; but there can be no such
thing. Religion is the most plain, simple
thing in the world ; it is only, We love Him
because He first loved us." But when Wesley
began to have doubts about Law's presentation
of Christianity, and wrote a letter setting out
his objections, Law answered with a scathing
politeness which was enough to terminate
any friendship. Wesley, however, retained
his admiration for much of Law's writings
till the last. It would have been better for
Law to associate with men of such power
as Wesley, instead of with the two estimable

but rather weak women who sat at his feet in the last part of his life.

The treatise entitled, *A Serious Call to a Devout and Holy Life; adapted to the State and Condition of All Orders of Christians*, was written at this time. It is a tremendous indictment of lukewarmness in religion, a ruthless exposure of the sin and folly of trying to make the best of both worlds. It is especially addressed to the leisured class, among whom this type of character is perhaps most common. The book well deserves its fame. The imaginary characters which he draws to illustrate his teaching are admirably sketched, with a profusion of wit and biting satire which delights the mind of the reader while it makes his conscience ashamed. We may say, by the way, that Gibbon's statement about two of the characters—that they are meant for his two aunts, "the heathen and the Christian sister"—cannot be true. Miss Hester Gibbon may have tried to copy "Miranda," but Miranda was not copied from her, nor Flavia from her sister. The most beautiful of all the character-sketches, that of the model country parson, Ouranius, represents the ideal which Law himself tried to realise, and from all accounts he did not fall far short of it. Ouranius, "when he first entered Holy Orders, had a great contempt for all foolish and unreasonable people ; but he has prayed this spirit away. When he first came to his little village, it was as disagreeable to him as a prison ; and every day seemed too tedious to be endured in so retired a place. His parish was full of poor and mean people that were none of them fit for the conversation of a gentleman. He kept much at home, writ notes upon Homer and Plautus, and sometimes thought it hard to be called to pray by any poor body, when he was just in the midst of one of Homer's battles. But now his days are so far from being tedious, or his parish too great a retirement, that he wants only more time to do that variety of good which his soul thirsts after. . . . He now thinks the poorest creature in the parish good enough, and great enough, to deserve the humblest attendances, the

kindest friendships, the tenderest offices, he
can possibly show them. He is so far now
from wanting agreeable company, that he
thinks there is no better conversation in the
world, than to be talking with poor and mean
people about the Kingdom of God. . . . He
loves every soul in the parish as he loves
himself, because he prays for them all as he
prays for himself."

There is much more of the same kind.
Not even George Herbert has drawn a more
winning picture of what the pastoral life was
meant to be and may be. The influence of
the *Serious Call* was both immediate and
lasting. John Wesley describes it as "a
treatise which will hardly be excelled, if it
be equalled, in the English tongue, either for
beauty of expression, or for justness and depth
of thought." Samuel Johnson called it "the
finest piece of hortatory theology in any
language," and says that his first reading of
it "was the first occasion of my thinking in
earnest." Gibbon says of it : "His precepts
are rigid, but they are founded on the Gospel.
His satire is sharp ; but it is drawn from the

knowledge of human life, and many of his portraits are not unworthy of the pen of La Bruyère. If he finds a spark of piety in his reader's mind, he will soon fan it into a flame ; and a philosopher must allow that he exposes, with equal severity and truth, the strange contradiction between the faith and practice of the Christian world." Gibbon feels, as none can fail to do, the extreme severity of Law's presentment of Christianity. The book is just what its title promises, a serious call—there is not much of the joy and peace in believing to be found in its pages. For that very reason, at the present day, when divines are offering us religion without tears, salvation without self-sacrifice, Law's treatise should be studied prayerfully by all who care for their soul's health.

It was about the year 1734 when Law first became acquainted with the writings of the German mystic, sometimes called the "Teutonic philosopher," Jacob Böhme. His study of them was destined to colour all the rest of his life. I have already mentioned his early attraction to the mystics, and his

study of Malebranche. The controversies in
which he engaged after leaving Cambridge
partially diverted his attention from the subject,
though he continued to read Tauler and other
mystical writers. But Böhme stirred him to
the very depths. The illuminated cobbler of
Gorlitz, who was born in 1575, was indeed
a religious genius of no ordinary kind. His
visions, which were sometimes induced by
self-hypnotisation, Böhme gazing fixedly at
the light shining through his door, till he
lost consciousness of the external world, are
incoherent enough in form, and are mixed
with the wildest fantasies. But those who
have patience enough will find in them, as
Schlegel did, "a fullness of fancy and depth
of feeling, a charm of nature, simplicity, and
unsought vigour," combined with real intellectual and speculative power, which have
earned for him a very honourable place
in the history both of religious philosophy
and of German literature. The fact that Sir
Isaac Newton, as well as William Law, was
a student of Böhme, should be enough to
preserve his name from the contempt which

s

some writers have lavished upon him. But
before discussing Law's later theology, from
the time when he fell under this new influence,
I wish to complete the story of his uneventful
life.

On the death of the elder Gibbon, in 1738
or 1739, the house at Putney was broken up,
and at the end of 1740 Law returned to his
native village of King's Cliffe, where his
brother George had a house. There he was
soon joined by Mrs Hutcheson, now a widow,
and Miss Hester Gibbon. The three lived
together in a comfortable house near the
church, and endeavoured to put into practice
the precepts of the *Serious Call.* The
ladies were rich, and the united incomes of
the three amounted to £3000 a year, nine-
tenths of which was deliberately devoted to
charity. Their manner of life was simple,
but not ascetic; Law himself lived mainly in
two rooms, well furnished with books, and
spent the greater part of each day in reading
and writing. Their charities, unfortunately,
were managed without discretion. It was an
age of reckless giving, as the light literature

of the Georgian age shows plainly; and none of the three had much practical wisdom. King's Cliffe became such a hunting-ground for vagrants that the rector and other parishioners were driven to protest. A saint who could never resist the impulse to liberate imprisoned canaries from their cages, to fall a prey to the nearest cat, was not the best financial adviser for two rich and not very clear - headed women. In all other ways Law's life was most exemplary. His peaceful and happy residence at King's Cliffe was only terminated by his death, at the age of seventy-five, in 1761. The two ladies both survived him, and reached the ages of eighty-five and ninety.

It is now time to turn to Law's later theology, in virtue of which he holds a prominent place among English mystical writers. And first, a few words must be said about the opinions of Jacob Böhme, whose disciple he professed himself. Böhme was a self - taught philosopher, who, besides the Bible, was acquainted only with the older Protestant mystics, and with the eccentric

genius Paracelsus who is the subject of
Robert Browning's earliest great poem. The
characteristic feature of the older Protestant
mysticism was a revolt against forensic
doctrines of the Atonement. "It is a note-
worthy error of false Christians," says Valentine
Weigel, "that they leave another to obey
the law, to suffer, and to die; while they
desire, without repentance, to avail themselves
of imputed righteousness. Nay, truly, thou
canst have no help from outside! That must
come from the Christ within thee, not from
one who is outside. True faith is the life of
Christ in us; it is being baptized with Him,
suffering, dying, and rising again with Him.
Christ's death and merits are imputed to no
one, unless he have Christ's death in himself,
and unless he rise with Him to a new life."
This deeply moral and spiritual view of
salvation, combined with the fantastic speculations of Paracelsus, is the foundation of
Böhme's theology, which, however, also contains Neoplatonic elements, derived we know
not whence, but presumably from the school
of Eckhart. God, the Eternal Father, is

described as the Abyss, as pure Will, in
which all things lie unexpressed. The Son
is the Eternal Good, which the Father dis-
covers and gives birth to within Himself.
The Son is the reality, the actualisation, of
the Divine nature. The office of the Holy
Spirit, within the bosom of the Godhead, is
as a bond between the Father and Son,
and the expression of their joint life. In the
world of existence, nothing can become
manifest to itself without *contrariness*. The
abysmal Will in the beginning *divided* itself,
that it might have a sphere in which to
work. This is the law of all existence. "In
Yes and No all things consist." The "No"
is a countercheck to the "Yes," without which
the truth, or God, would be unknowable and
inoperative. There is no day without night,
no heat without cold, no joy without longing.
So the Divine nature differentiates itself into
love and anger, heaven and hell. The visible
world is a counterpart of the spiritual, which
God made out of His own substance. It is
the living garment of God, as Goethe says.
"When thou lookest on the firmament and

the stars and the earth," says Böhme, "thou
seest thy God, in whom thou also livest and
hast thy being. If this whole sphere of
existence be not God, thou art not God's
image. If there be anywhere a God foreign
to it, thou hast no part in Him." Evil is
the necessary condition of the activity of
good. " Love submits to the fire of wrath
that it may be itself a fire of love." Good
can only exist by turning sorrow into joy,
by overcoming opposition and harmonising
discord. Thus by a fanciful etymology he
says that quality, determination (*Qual*) is
inseparable from suffering (*Quaal*). The path
of salvation is the conquest and renunciation
of the self-will which separates us from the
will of God. We desire to know nothing
further about God than what God chooses to
know in and through us. The whole frame-
work of his religion is contained in the
following account of his experiences. " I am
not a master of literature or the arts, but
a foolish and simple man. I have never
desired learning, but from early youth I
strove after the salvation of my soul, and

thought how I might inherit the Kingdom of
Heaven. Finding within myself a powerful
contrariness, namely, the desires that belong
to flesh and blood, I began to fight a hard
battle against my corrupted nature, and with
the help of God made up my mind to overcome the inherited evil will, to break it, and
to enter wholly into the love of God in Christ.
I therefore resolved henceforth to regard
myself as dead in my inherited form, until
the Spirit of God should be formed in me,
so that in and through Him I might conduct
my life. This I could not accomplish, but
I stood firmly by my resolution, and fought
a hard battle with myself. While I was
thus wrestling and battling, being aided by
God, a wonderful light arose within my soul.
It was a light quite unlike my unruly
nature, but I recognised in it the true
nature of God and man, a thing which
I had never before understood or sought
for."

Characteristic mystical sayings gleaned from
his works are the following :—

"If you will behold your own self and the outer world,

you will find that you yourself, with regard to your external being, are that external world."

"It is not I who know these things, but God knows them in me."

"When thou canst throw thyself for a moment into that where no creature dwelleth, then thou hearest what God speaketh."

"He that findeth love findeth God; and he that findeth God findeth nothing and all things."

"The soul hath heaven and hell within itself."

"The body of a man is the visible world, and the visible world is a manifestation of the inner spiritual world; it is a copy of eternity, wherewith eternity hath made itself visible."

These views place Böhme in the main line of development of German thought which culminated in Schelling and Hegel, and also, through his insistence on Will as the constitutive principle of the world, make him a precursor of Schopenhauer. William Law does not adopt his system in its entirety. He is less of an intellectualist than Böhme, in spite of his much wider reading. The parts of Böhme which attracted him most were the polemic against forensic doctrines of the Atonement; the perpetual insistence that God is love, and that wrath is foreign to His nature, the doctrine of the *unio mystica*

brought, as with St Paul, into closest connection with Christology; and the analogy
between the visible and invisible world, the
sacramental view of life.   These doctrines
were not borrowed from Böhme.   Law believed
them before.   But in the Teutonic philosopher
he found for the first time an illuminating
exposition of his own deepest convictions;
and the result was a new note in his teaching,
a note of ardent and rapturous emotion, which
blends in the most striking manner with the
old austerity and moralism.   Law's later
books contain some of the noblest and
strongest writing in the literature of devotion,
whether in our own language or in any other.

Students of Law's theology should give
particular attention to a short essay called
*The Grounds and Reasons of Christian
Regeneration*, which the author himself
referred to as containing the heads of
his teaching.   The following extracts are
characteristic: "What is it that any thoughtful, serious man could wish for but to
have a new heart and a new spirit, free
from the hellish self-tormenting elements

T

of selfishness, envy, pride, and wrath? His own experience has shown him that nothing human can do this for him; and it is so natural for him to think that God alone can do it, that he has often been tempted to accuse God for suffering it to be so with him. Therefore to have the Son of God come from heaven to redeem him, and to redeem him by way of regeneration, by a seed of His Divine nature sown into him must be a way of salvation highly suited to his own sense, wants and experience, because he finds that his evil lies deep in the very essence and forms of his nature, and therefore can only be removed by the arising of a new birth or life in the first essences of it. Therefore an inward Saviour, a Saviour that is God Himself, raising His own Divine birth in the human soul, has such a fitness in it as must make every sober man with open arms ready and willing to receive such a salvation.

" Some people have an idea of the Christian religion as if God was thereby declared so full of wrath against fallen man, that nothing but the blood of His only-begotten Son could satisfy his vengeance. Nay, some have gone such lengths of wickedness as to assert that God hath by immutable decrees reprobated a great part of the race of Adam to an inevitable damnation, to show forth and magnify the glory of His justice. But these are miserable mistakers of the Divine nature, and miserable reproachers of His great love and goodness in the Christian dispensation. For God is love, yea, all love, and so all love that nothing but love can come from Him; and the Christian religion is nothing else but an open, full manifestation of His universal love to all mankind. There is no wrath that stands between God and us, but what is awakened in the dark fire of our own fallen nature; and to quench this wrath, and not his own, God gave his only-begotten Son to be made man. The precious blood of His Son was not poured out to pacify Himself, who in Himself had no nature toward man but love; but it was poured out to quench the wrath and fire of the fallen soul, and kindle in it a birth of light and love."

Regeneration does not signify only a moral change of our inclinations. "Tempers and inclinations are the fruits of the new-born nature, and not the nature itself. Our nature must first be made good, its root and stock must be new made, before it can bring forth good fruits of moral behaviour. . . . The whole nature of the Christian religion stands upon these two great pillars, namely, the greatness of our fall, and the greatness of our redemption. Every one is necessarily more or less of a true penitent, and more or less truly converted to God, according as he is more or less inwardly sensible of these truths."

"No son of Adam is without a Saviour, or can be lost, but by his own turning away from this Saviour within him, and giving himself up to the suggestions and workings of the evil nature that is in him."

"A bare historical and superficial faith cannot save the soul, but leaves it a slave to sin." Human reason may assent to the truth that Christ is our Saviour, while "little or nothing is done to the soul by it; the soul

is under much the same power of sin as
before, because only the notion or image or
history of the truth is taken in by it; and
reason of itself can take in no more. But
when the seed of the new birth, called the
inward man, has faith awakened in it, its
faith is not a notion, but a real strong
hunger, which lays hold on Christ, puts on
the divine nature, and effectually works out
our salvation." We must beware not to
"make a saint of the natural man." Persons
of this stamp, Law truly observes, often over-
look in themselves errors of moral behaviour
such as the first beginners in religion dare
not allow themselves in. "There is nothing
safe in religion, but in such a course as
leaves nothing for corrupt nature to feed
or live upon."

How can a man know that he is in the
way of regeneration? Not by assurance that
he cannot fall from the state of grace. Such
confidence may be given by God to those
who need it, but normally what we want to
know is that we are alive and growing,
not that our salvation is secure. The

characters of saints differ widely. "Every complexion of the inward man, when sanctified by humility, and suffering itself to be turned and struck and moved by the Holy Spirit of God, according to its particular frame and turn, helps mightily to increase that harmony of Divine praise, thanksgiving, and adoration, which must arise from different instruments, sounds, and voices."

Law then attacks again the doctrine of assurance. "If I have not this gift of God, until my own feeling and assurance confirms it to me, I am self-justified, because my justification arises from what I feel and declare of myself." Strong impressions and delightful sensations in the spiritual life are gifts of God, but they should be classed with outward blessings, such as health and prosperity. "A soul may be as fully fixed in selfishness through a fondness of sensible enjoyments in spiritual things, as by a fondness for earthly satisfactions." "These inward delights are not holiness, they are not piety, they are not perfection, but they are God's gracious allurements and calls to seek after

holiness and perfection." " They ought rather
to convince us that we are as yet but babes,
than that we are really men of God." " The
soul is only so far cleansed from its corruption,
so far delivered from the power of sin, and
so far purified, as it has renounced all its
own will and desire, to have nothing, receive
nothing, and be nothing, but what the one
will of God chooses for it, and does to it.
This and this alone is the true Kingdom of
God opened in the soul." " There is nothing
evil, or the cause of evil to either man or
devil, but his own will ; there is nothing good
in itself, but the will of God." " Conversion
to God is often sudden, but this suddenness
is by no means of the essence of true conversion, and is neither to be demanded in
ourselves, nor required of others. The
purification of our souls is not a thing done
in an instant, but is a certain process, a
gradual release from our captivity and
disorder, consisting of several stages and
degrees, both of death and life, which the
soul must go through, before it can have
thoroughly put off the old man. Jesus

Christ is our pattern, and what He did for
us, we are also to do for ourselves." Our
Saviour's greatest trials were near the end
of His life : this should warn us not to be
self-assured of our own salvation. To sum
up : our own will is our separation from
God. "All the disorder and malady of our
nature lies in a certain fixedness of our own
will, imagination, and desires, wherein we
live to ourselves, are our own centre and
circumference, act wholly from ourselves,
according to our own will, imagination, and
desires. There is not the smallest degree
of evil in us, but what arises from this selfishness, because we are thus all in all to
ourselves. . . . It is enough for us to know
that we hunger and thirst after the righteousness which is in Christ Jesus ; that by faith
we desire and hope to be in Him new
creatures ; to know that the greatest humility,
the most absolute resignation of our whole
selves to God, is our greatest and highest
fitness to receive our greatest and highest
purification from the hands of God."

I know no better summary of the theology

and ethics of Christian mysticism than this
short treatise. Those persons who connect
mysticism with vague sentiment and luxurious
emotions should reconsider their opinion in
the light of this last paragraph. Those who
hunger and thirst after righteousness will
find consolations in mysticism ; those who
think to embrace mysticism for the sake of
its consolations will receive no encouragement
from the great mystics. "*Entbehren sollst
du, sollst entbehren,*" is the watchword that
is ever on their lips. If we would save
our souls, we must first surrender them
unconditionally.

I cannot refrain from quoting a magnificent
outburst of moral indignation from Law's next
controversial work, an answer to a discourse
"On the Folly, Sin, and Danger of being
Righteous Overmuch," by Dr Trapp, a typical
eighteenth-century divine. Trapp had even
ventured to appeal to our Blessed Lord's
example in support of his thesis. " O holy
Jesus!" Law exclaims, "that Thy Divine life
should, by a preacher of Thy Gospel, be
made a plea for liberties of indulgence! . . .

U

Our Saviour, suitable to His gracious love, in coming into the world, sought the conversation of publicans and sinners, because He came to save that which was lost, and because He knew that some among such sinners were more moveable than the proud sanctity of the learned Pharisees. . . . O holy Jesus! Thou didst nothing of Thyself, Thou soughtest only the glory of Thy Father from the beginning to the end of Thy life; Thou spentest whole nights in prayer on mountains and desert places; Thou hadst not where to lay Thy head; Thy common poor fare with Thy disciples was barely bread and dried fish; Thy miraculous power never helped Thee to any dainties of refreshment, though ever so much fatigued and fainted with labour. And yet because this holy Jesus came into the world to save all sorts of sinners, therefore He came into all places and entered into all sorts of companies. . . . It is said that wherever the king is, there is the court, but with much more reason may it be said, that whereever our Saviour came there was the Temple, or the Church. As He was

everywhere God, so every place became holy
to Him."

In an answer to an angry rejoinder by Dr
Trapp, who had called Law an "enthusiast"
—a favourite term of vituperation in the
eighteenth century — he boldly accepts the
word. "Enthusiasm is as common, as
universal, as essential to human nature as
love is. No people are so angry with
religious enthusiasts as those who are the
deepest in some enthusiasm of another kind.
He who travels over high mountains to salute
the dear ground that Cicero walked upon,
whose noble soul would be ready to break
out of his body if he could see a desk from
which Cicero had poured forth his thunder
of words, may well be unable to bear the
dullness of those who go on pilgrimages only
to visit the sepulchre whence the Saviour of
the world rose from the dead, or who grow
devout at the sight of a crucifix, because the
Son of God hung as a sacrifice thereon. . . .
Even the poor species of fops and beaux
have a right to be placed among enthusiasts,
though capable of no other flame than that

which is kindled by tailors and peruke-makers. Enthusiasm is not blameable in religion when it is true religion that kindles it. . . . Every man, as such, has an open gate to God in his soul; he is always in that temple, where he can worship God in spirit and in truth. Every Christian, as such, has the firstfruits of the Spirit, a seed of life, which is his call and qualification to be always in a state of inward prayer, faith, and holy intercourse with God. All the ordinances of the Gospel, the daily sacramental service of the Church, is to keep up and exercise and strengthen this faith; to raise us to such an habitual faith · and dependence upon the light and Holy Spirit of God, that by thus seeking and finding God in the institutions of the Church, we may be habituated to seek Him and find Him, to live in His light, and walk by His Spirit in all the actions of our ordinary life. This is the enthusiasm in which every good Christian ought to endeavour to live and die."

Canon Overton, in commenting on this passage, asks, "Is it possible that this man could have lived in the eighteenth century?"

The high sacramental doctrine, the contempt for grammarians and critics, the unabashed defence of enthusiasm, seem to belong to any age rather than the generation of Warburton, Hoadly, Sherlock, and Butler. The isolation of Law as a thinker both explains the partial neglect in which he lived, and increases our admiration for his originality and courage.

The two most charming of Law's mystical works are *The Spirit of Prayer* and *The Spirit of Love*, published between 1749 and 1752. The former, however, is somewhat marred by the extreme anti-intellectualism which was part of Law's later philosophy. It was a reaction against the rationalism of the Deists and their opponents, who combated Deism with its own weapons. One of the interlocutors in the dialogue (for *The Spirit of Prayer* is cast in this form), whom Law calls Academicus, describes how when he began to study divinity, some advised him to learn Hebrew, others Greek; others told him that Church history is the main matter; "that I must begin with the lives of the first Fathers, not forgetting the lives of the Roman emperors." "Another, who is wholly bent on rational Christianity, tells me that I need go no higher than the Reformation. . . . My tutor is very liturgical; he has some suspicion that our Sacrament of the Lord's Supper is essentially defective, for want of a little water in the wine. . . . The last friend I consulted advised me to get all the histories of the rise and progress of heresies, and to be well versed in the casuists and schoolmen. This knowledge, he said, might be useful to me when I came to be a parish priest." Academicus, when he has found "the true way of Divine knowledge," regards all these investigations as lost labour. I must return, at the close of this Lecture, to Law's hostile attitude towards human reason.

The Spirit of Love, which in my opinion is Law's masterpiece, deals with the two objections, that Love is too ethereal a principle for practical life, and that the Bible represents God as a jealous and even a wrathful Being. He begins by saying that God, as considered in Himself, is "only an eternal Will to all goodness." "As certainly as He is the Creator, so certainly is He the Blesser, of every created thing, and can give nothing but blessing, goodness, and happiness from Himself, because He has in Himself nothing else to give." This is the ground and original of the spirit of love in the creature—it is and must be a Will to all goodness. The spirit of love, wherever it is, is its own blessing and happiness, because it is the truth and reality of God in the soul. "Oh, sir," he exclaims, "would you know the blessing of all blessings, it is this God of love dwelling in your soul, and killing every root of bitterness, which is the pain and torment of every earthly, selfish love. For all wants are satisfied, all disorders of nature are removed, no life is any longer a burden, every day is a day of peace, everything you meet becomes a help to you, because everything you see or do is all done in the sweet, gentle element of love. The spirit of love does not want to be rewarded, honoured, or esteemed; its only desire is to propagate itself, and become the blessing and happiness of everything that wants it." It meets evil as the light meets the darkness, only to overcome it.

Christ can never be in any creature, except
as the spirit of love. Whenever, therefore,
we willingly indulge wrath or hatred, we are
actively resisting Christ; we do what the
Jews did, when they said, "We will not
have this man to reign over us."

All evil and misery are the result of man's
will being turned from God; for whatever
wills and works with God must partake of
this happiness and perfection. We are all
fallen creatures, who crave and strive for
purification, and restoration to the spirit of
love.

Then follows an exposition of Böhme's
theories about body and soul, the most
interesting part of which is the conclusion
that "body and spirit are not two separate,
independent things, but are necessary to each
other, and are only the inward and outward
conditions of one and the same being."
Passages like this explain the charge of
"Spinozism" brought against Law by Warburton—an accusation which Law repudiated
with unusual heat, holding that "Spinozism
is nothing else but a gross confounding of

God and nature." Spinozism is, of course, a great deal more than this; but Law does not seem to have really studied Spinoza.

The rationalism of the Deists is next attacked. "Reason" can no more alter the life of the soul than the life of the body. He only who can say to the dead body of Lazarus, "Come forth," can say to the soul, "Be thou clean." Logic cannot make a man a moral philosopher. We must not put our eyes to do the work of our hands and feet. The spirit of love is a spirit of nature and life, not a creation or discovery of the intellect. It is as surely real as health and strength, it is a form or state of life. In this paragraph Law approaches what is now called pragmatism. As against the shallow rationalism and common-sense philosophy of the Deists, he is right, but our distrust of reasons should not prejudice us against reason, with which religion has no quarrel.

The doctrine of the Cross is the necessity of dying to self, as the only way to life in God. "This is the one morality that does man any good. There are only two possible

X

states of life : the one is nature, and the other is God manifested in nature. We must choose one or the other. We cannot stand still without deciding, for 'life goes on, and is always bringing forth its realities, which way soever it goeth.'" Here speaks the author of the *Serious Call*; after much fantastic Behmenism, it is a relief to catch the tone of the stern English moralist once more.

The "Second Part" of *The Spirit of Love* is in the form of a dialogue between Theogenes, Eusebius, and Theophilus. All nature, says Theophilus, is what it is, for this only end, that the hidden riches of the unsearchable God may become manifest in and by it. God's unchangeable disposition towards His creatures is only the communication of His own love, goodness, and happiness to them, according to their capacities. He can no more *become* angry with His creatures, than *be* angry with them at first. God's *pity* is not the beginning of a new temper ; it is a new manifestation of His eternal will to all goodness ; but to suppose that God feels wrath and fury, because the poor creature

has brought misery upon itself, is impious
and absurd. Wrath is always a corrupt and
disordered state; it is so in man, and could
not be otherwise in God. Wrath, therefore,
can no more be in God Himself than hell
can be heaven. The creature experiences
wrath and misery by losing the living presence
of the Spirit of God; for no intelligent creature
can be good and happy but by partaking of a
twofold life. The natural life is a life of
various appetites, hungers, and wants, and
cannot be anything else; it can go no higher
than a bare capacity for goodness, and cannot
be a good and happy life, but by the life of
God dwelling in, and in union with it. Hence
the necessity for the Incarnation. The union
of the Divine and human life, to make man
again a partaker of the Divine nature, is the
only possible salvation for man. All salvation
is, and can be nothing else, but the manifestation of the life of God in the soul. All
particular dispensations, whether by the law
or the prophets, by the Scriptures, or
ordinances of the Church, are only helps to
a holiness which they cannot give. Perpetual

inspiration, by the immediate indwelling, union, and operation of the Deity in the life of the creature, is not fanaticism, or enthusiasm, but a thing as necessary to a life of goodness as the perpetual respiration of the air is necessary to animal life. What a mistake it is to confine inspiration to particular times and occasions, to prophets and apostles and extraordinary messengers of God! We are not all called to be apostles or prophets, but all are called to be holy, as He who has called us is holy. The holiness of the Christian is not an occasional thing, nor, on the other hand, is it ever his own work; he must therefore be continually inspired.

Law then makes his own the old mystical doctrine of the spark of heaven hidden in the soul. "If Christ was to raise a new life like His own in every man, then every man must have had originally in the inmost spirit of his life, a seed of Christ, or Christ as a seed of heaven, lying there as in a state of insensibility or death, out of which it could not arise, but by the mediatorial power of Christ. Unless there was this seed of Christ,

no beginning of Christ's mediatorial office
could be made. For what could begin to
deny self, if there was not in man something
different from self? Unless all the command-
ments had been really in the soul, in vain
had the tables of stone been given to man.
And unless Christ lay in the soul, as its
unknown, hidden treasure, as a seed of life,
a power of salvation, in vain had the holy
Jesus lived and died for man. The redeeming
work of Christ is to raise the smothered spark
of heaven out of its state of death, into a
powerful governing life of the whole man.
And you, says Law's Theophilus, need no
other deliverance, but from the power of
your own earthly self. It is your own Cain
that murders your own Abel. Daily and
hourly see to the spirit that is within you,
whether it is heaven or earth that guides
you. Do not cross the seas to find a new
Luther or a new Calvin, to clothe yourself
with their opinions. No, the oracle is at
home, that always and only speaks the truth
to you. Salvation or damnation is no outward
thing, that is brought into you from without,

but is only that which springs up within
you, as the birth and state of your own life.
What you are in yourself, what is doing in
yourself, is all that can be either your salvation or damnation. "Your salvation precisely
consists, not in any historic faith, or knowledge of anything absent or distant from you,
not in any variety of restraints, rules, and
methods of practising virtues, not in any
formality of opinion about faith and works,
repentance, forgiveness of sins, or justification
and sanctification, but wholly · and solely in
the life of God, or Christ of God, quickened,
and born again in you."

The atonement of the Divine wrath, and
the extinguishing of sin, are but two names
for the same thing. The atonement made no
change in the mind of God, but overcame
and removed all the death and hell and
wrath and darkness, which had opened itself
in the nature, birth, and life of fallen man.
Transactional theories of the atonement, Law
argues, are not really scriptural. When the
Bible says that righteousness, or justice, is
satisfied by the atonement of Christ, it means

that strict righteousness or justice has its absolute demands on man, which it cannot relax. Christ takes away the sins of the world by restoring to man his lost righteousness. He gave Himself for the Church, that He might sanctify and cleanse it. Man's original righteousness has become his tormentor, and must plague him until it is restored to him. God's chastisements are all for our good. "If the holy Jesus had been wanting in severity, He had been wanting in true love."

"There is nothing that is supernatural," says Law, "in the whole system of our redemption. Every part of it has its ground in the workings and powers of nature, and all our redemption is only nature set right, or made to be that which it ought to be. There is nothing that is supernatural, but God alone; everything beside Him is subject to the state of nature. There is nothing supernatural in the mystery of our redemption, but the supernatural love and wisdom which brought it forth." "The Christian religion is the only true religion of nature; it has nothing in it supernatural."

"Nothing can be done to any creature super-naturally, or in a way that is without, or contrary to, the powers of nature." "A religion is not to be deemed natural, because it has nothing to do with revelation; but then it is the one true religion of nature, when it has everything in it that our natural state stands in need of."

I will conclude my extracts from *The Spirit of Love* with these words, omitting an interesting discussion upon the source of sin and misery, in the last dialogue. It will not be necessary to comment upon the few writings which belong to the last years of Law's life. His last written words, indited a few days before his death, contain the kernel of his theology. "All that Christ was, did, suffered, dying in the flesh, and ascending into heaven, was for this sole end: to purchase for all His followers a new birth, new life, and new light, in and by the Spirit of God restored to them, and living in them, as their support, comforter, and guide into all truth. And this was His, 'Lo, I am with you alway, even unto the end of the world.'"

William Law expounds the principles of Christian Mysticism in a peculiarly sound and attractive form. The only defects, as it seems to me, in his later writings are his adoption of some of the more fantastic theories of Böhme, and his extreme anti-intellectualism. He ignores Plato and the Platonists, though he has very much in common with them. It is remarkable that an Emmanuel man should show so little sympathy with Cambridge Platonism, of which his own College was the nursery. One would have supposed that in the writings of John Smith, Benjamin Whichcote, Henry More, and Cudworth, Law would have found a great deal to admire and very little to disapprove. It is true that Law was a High Churchman, while the Cambridge group were already nicknamed "Latitudinarians" and "rational theologians." But this should not have been fatal to an understanding between kindred spirits. The truth seems to be, that Law was well acquainted with More alone in this group; and though he admired his character, he regarded him as an adversary of the "inner

Y

light," and his books as "a jumble of learned
rant," which some of them certainly are.
In John Smith he might have found a
rationalism in no way antagonistic to his
own mysticism—a religious philosophy more
complete and not less devout than his own,
based not on the dreams of an illuminated
cobbler, but on the thoughts of Plato and
Plotinus, Christianised by a saint who was
also a scholar. A very few sentences from
the discourses of this gifted young theologian
will show how much affinity there was between
him and Law. "Such as men themselves are,
such will God Himself seem to be." "He
that will find truth, must seek it with a free
judgment and a sanctified mind. He that
thus seeks shall find; he shall live in truth,
and that shall live in him. He shall drink
of the waters of his own cistern, and be
satisfied. He shall find satisfaction within,
feeling himself in conjunction with truth,
though all the world should dispute against
him." "When men most of all fly from
God, they still seek after Him." "God is
not better defined to us by our under-

standings, than by our wills and affections."
" Divinity is a Divine life rather than a
Divine science—the fear of the Lord is the
beginning of wisdom." The true life of the
Christian " is nothing else but an infant
Christ formed in his soul." " Heaven is
not a thing without us, nor is happiness
anything distinct from a true conjunction of
the mind with God." " God does not bid us
be warmed and filled, and deny us those
necessities which our starving and hungry
souls call for." " I doubt sometimes that we
make the unspotted righteousness of Christ a
covering wherein to wrap our foul deformities,
and when we have done, think that we are
become Heaven's darlings as much as we are
our own." Most of these maxims are quite
in accordance with Law's sentiments; but
Smith is superior to Law in his claim that
the " Reason" must not be scouted as the
source of a frigid Deism, but given its rightful
place in the hierarchy of our faculties. Smith
is far too much of a mystic to be a rationalist;
but he is also far too good a Platonist to
think that mental cultivation is no help towards

right belief and right living.   These two noble thinkers should both be read by all who wish to know the best that Anglican theology has produced.   It has not been the interest of either of our two militant parties to republish them; but they are far more worthy to live than certain other books which have been disinterred in the cause of faction.   A study of the *Serious Call*, *The Spirit of Love*, or Smith's *Select Discourses*, may not make the reader a better Catholic or a better Protestant, but they cannot fail to make him a better Christian and a better man.

LECTURE V

THE MYSTICISM OF WORDSWORTH

In using a poet as a religious teacher, we must remember that the object of poetry is beauty, not truth or edification, and that to forget this leads to bad criticism. As William Watson says :

" Forget not, brother singer, that though Prose
    Can never be too truthful, nor too wise,
  Song is not Truth nor Wisdom, but the rose
    Upon Truth's lips, the light in Wisdom's eyes."

Still, our generation has chosen to go to the poets for moral teaching, even more than to its professional instructors ; and I do not know that it is mistaken. What Horace says of Homer is true of most great poets :

" Quid sit pulcrum, quid turpe, quid utile, quid non,
  Rectius et melius Chrysippo et Crantore dicit."

And, besides, less violence is done to a poet

in seeking in him for a mystical interpretation of life, than for a scheme of morality. For if it is the essence of mysticism to believe that everything, in being what it is, is symbolic of something higher and deeper than itself, mysticism is, on one side, the poetry of life. For poetry also consists in finding resemblances ; to be good at metaphors is, as Aristotle says, the most important part of poetic diction. Poetry also universalises the particulars with which it deals ; it treats the particular thing as a microcosm, an image in little of "what God and man is." From the matter-of-fact point of view, "all poetry," like all mysticism, "is misrepresentation"—a dictum of Jeremy Bentham. So Shakespeare makes Audrey talk to Touchstone about poetry. "I do not know what 'poetical' is. Is it honest in deed and word? Is it a true thing?" Yes, we may answer; it is a true thing; but poetry has its own canons of truthfulness, which are not those of science, nor of the matter-of-fact world. It is not the primary object of the poet to give us information, nor to preach to us.

But though we have had quite enough essays
on this and that poet "as a religious teacher,"
no apology is needed for treating Wordsworth
in this way.   He wished to be treated in
this way.   "I wish either to be considered
as a teacher," he said, "or as nothing."
Moreover, his worth as a moralist has been
proved.   We take him down from the shelf
sometimes when we are in trouble—a compli-
ment which is paid to very few of the great
classics.   Why is this?   Because Wordsworth
has a definite philosophy of life, and an ethical
system which is capable of being made a
principle of conduct.   He is a practical
counsellor.   If we will take him as our
guide, he will show us a path which he at
least followed to the end, and reached his
goal.   It may not suit everybody, but it has
been proved to suit some people.

The phrase "natural religion," or "the
religion of nature," has been used to cover
many different phases of religious belief.
The recognition of a divine revelation in all
phenomena was a very early form of religion.
But in its earlier forms it offered an extremely

crude and summary solution of the problem of evil—by denying its existence. In primitive Oriental pantheism all is equally divine. God is "as full, as perfect, in a hair as heart," as Pope puts it. We shall see that Wordsworth rises above this superficial view. He has also hardly anything in common with the "natural" evidential theology of which Paley is the best known exponent, a type of apologetics on which we may surely pass sentence in Bacon's words, that "it suffices to confute atheism, but not to inform religion." The weakness of this school, besides its police-court method of weighing evidences, is its extreme anthropocentric bias — humanity is made the centre round which the whole universe revolves ; which seems not to be true.

Nor can we find Wordsworth's true precursors in the Platonists, who regarded natural beauty, including that of the human form, as the chief hierophant of the heavenly mysteries. Plato represents true beauty not as earthly, perishable, and sensuous, but as heavenly, immortal, and spiritual. Dwelling in the nature of God, it imparts grace by emanations and gleams of loveliness to all that is beautiful in this lower world; and it is by communion with this spiritual essence revealing itself in forms of earthly beauty to pure and loving hearts and chaste imaginations, that the mind of man is cleansed and sanctified and spiritualised, and has visions of God and the eternal "world of ideas."

"The perfection of beauty," says Winckelmann, a devout disciple of Plato, "exists only in God, and human beauty is elevated in proportion as it approaches the idea of God. This idea of beauty is a spiritual quintessence extracted from created substances, as it were, by an alchemy of fire; and is produced by the imagination endeavouring to conceive what is human as existing as a prototype in the mind of God." This is pure Platonism, as first expounded by Plato in the *Phaedrus*. We find it again in some of our great poets: in Spenser, for example, whom I quoted in my first Lecture as a nature-mystic of the Platonic school.

In Shelley the same note is struck, but with greater impatience for the transit from the

z

many to the One, from the visible to the invisible beauty.

We do not catch the true Wordsworthian tone in Plato or his numerous disciples. It is not the *beauty* of nature which Wordsworth finds most elevating. Not the sense of beauty, but of eternal and ubiquitous *life*— of an universe animated throughout, and obeying one law — this thought, which is rather Stoical than Platonic, is most prominent in Wordsworth. It will be one of the chief subjects of this Lecture to examine what are the moral and religious conclusions which follow from this way of regarding and contemplating the natural world.

The line of thought which must now occupy us is obviously very near what is called pantheism. There is, however, this great difference, that in pantheistic mysticism God is really everything; while in ordinary pantheism everything is God. This sentence is from Rothe, who adds quite truly that "the pantheism of the Middle Ages was a movement of moral contemplation in opposition to the purely religious : we find in it a dawning consciousness of the really Divine nature of ordinary created existence." There was, in fact, at the Renaissance, a revival of the doctrine of pan-psychism, which had slumbered since the Neoplatonists. It appears in Bruno, and in Campanella, from whom I quote a stanza in Symonds' translation :

> "Deem you that only you have thought and sense,
>   While heaven and all its wonders, sun, and earth,
>   Scorned in your dullness, lack intelligence?
> Fool! what produced you? These things gave you birth ;
>   So have they mind and God."

During the ascendency of the mechanical philosophy this doctrine passed under a cloud, from which it has now emerged. We need not call it pantheism, for a useful distinction has been expressed by the word "panentheism," or universal Divine immanence, in contrast with pantheism, or identity of the universe with God. True pantheism is, or must be while it is consistent, non-ethical; for if everything is equally Divine, or as Divine as its nature permits it to be, there can be no distinction between what is and what ought to be. Non-ethical pantheism tends on the

whole to be pessimistic, not because an
unbiassed outlook on the world really leads
to pessimism, but because it is an imperfect
and partly false view of reality, and, as such,
fails to satisfy the wants of the human heart.
It is only a few buoyant natures, such as
Emerson, who have found the thought
stimulating. We may compare his—

> "They reckon ill who leave me out;
>   When me they fly, I am the wings;
> I am the doubter and the doubt,
>   And I the hymn the Brahmin sings,"

with—

> "Ne suis-je pas un faux accord
>   Dans la divine symphonie,
>   Grâce à la vorace harmonie
> Qui me secoue et qui me mord?

> "Elle est dans ma voix, la criarde!
>   C'est tout mon sang, ce poison noir!
>   Je suis le sinistre miroir
> Où la mégère se regarde!

> "Je suis la plaie et le couteau!
>   Je suis le soufflet et la joue!
>   Je suis les membres et la roue,
> Et la victime et le bourreau!" [1]

This kind of pantheism has found many
adherents among those who think that the

---

[1] Quoted by Bradley, *Appearance and Reality*, p. 447.

trend of natural science is towards a rigid
determinism. It may take a theistic colour.
The irresistible Power which, on this theory,
determines all our actions, may be called
God, as by the Stoics, and may be the
object of worship. This kind of pantheistic
determinism is represented, among our poets,
by Shelley, not by Wordsworth. Shelley
says: "We live and move and think; but
we are not the creators of our own origin
and existence. We are not the arbiters of
every motion of our complicated nature; we
are not the masters of our own imagination
and moods of mental being. There is a
Power by which we are surrounded, like the
atmosphere in which some motionless lyre
is suspended, which visits with its breath our
silent chords at will. Our most imperial
qualities are the passive slaves of some
higher and more omnipotent Power. That
Power is God; and those who have seen
God have, in the period of their purer and
more perfect nature, been harmonised by
their own will to so exquisite a consentaneity
of power as to give forth divinest melody,

when the breath of universal Being sweeps over their frame." Samuel Taylor Coleridge, in an early poem, expresses the same view, and uses the same metaphor, in verse :

> " And what if all of animated nature
> Be but organic harps diversely framed,
> That tremble into thought as o'er them sweeps,
> Plastic and vast, one intellectual breeze
> At once the soul of each, and God of all ? "

Wordsworth, as we shall see, believes in law, but in *spiritual* law ; and spiritual law, though it acts uniformly, does not exclude, but expressly includes, the ideas of will and purpose.

I have said that the poet and the mystic seek to pass from the particular to the universal in much the same manner. Tennyson, in a familiar and often quoted stanza, says that if we could understand a tiny flower, peeping out of a cranny in a wall, we should know what God and man is. So Blake speaks of the aspiration :

> " To see a world in a grain of sand,
> And a heaven in a wild flower,
> Hold infinity in the palm of your hand
> And eternity in an hour."

Wordsworth himself quotes, with fond approbation, some beautiful lines of Wither, which are nearer to his own mind than those just cited from Blake :

> " By the murmur of a spring,
>   Or the least bough's rustelling ;
>   By a daisy, whose leaves spread
>   Shut when Titan goes to bed ;
>
> " Or a shady bush or tree—
>   She could more infuse in me
>   Than all Nature's beauties can
>   In some other wiser man."

" She," it must be explained, is Wither's muse, not his mistress.

But what are the lessons which these ambitious lines refer to as capable of being drawn from the smallest natural object or the most transitory of nature's effects ? We can only answer that men have found them almost infinitely diverse. Perhaps the earliest feelings inspired by nature were those of awe and fear, as of some mysterious and probably malevolent power. Others have drawn only the lesson of man's impotence and nature's ruthless destructiveness. Lucretius describes a Roman fleet, sailing from harbour in all the pomp

and splendour of war, bearing on board mighty
legions ; and then how a storm arises, and
how the general prays for help : "in vain, for
all none the less are carried down into the
waters of death."

"Nequiquam, quoniam violento turbine saepe
Correptus nilo fertur minus ad vada leti."

At other times in human history a sort of
passionate sympathy with the seasons—with
the destroying and renewing forces of nature
—has determined the character of a religion.
All those are far from Wordsworth's mind.
Nor does his teaching consist of a mere stock-
taking of nature's picturesque effects. It has
been said with much truth that there is no
scenery in Wordsworth. His stage is bare of
scenery, and contains only actors. We had
had picturesque description before Wordsworth, in James Thomson's *Seasons*, and
perhaps, as Wordsworth himself thought, in
Sir Walter Scott, who observed nature with
pencil and notebook in his hand. "Nature,"
said Wordsworth, in criticising this method,
"does not permit an inventory to be made
of her charms." The attitude of Words-

worth towards nature was neither a quest of picturesque effects, nor mere admiring admiration, nor a wish to find a background to the expression of human love and sorrow. All these ways of approaching nature had been trodden before him. Wordsworth's inspiration was something more original ; something which came direct to him ; a revelation of the unseen through natural objects, whereby he was granted the power to "see into the life of things." (Observe that it is the life, not the beauty of things, which becomes plain to him.) His poetry is, I think, the best example in literature of a revelation through impersonal external nature. Love, in the sense which the word bears in Browning's poetry, contributed little or nothing to his religious insight.

But there is one fact about Wordsworth's inspiration which cannot be emphasised too strongly. It came to him, in the sense that he did not borrow it; but it did not come unsought. It was prepared for and earned by a severe course of moral training. Let those who think that nature will yield her secrets to the holiday-maker who seeks rest, not from honest labour but from the busy idleness of London society, ponder these words of Novalis, another mystic, who has something in common with Wordsworth. "Let him who would arrive at the knowledge of nature train his moral sense; let him act and conceive in accordance with the noble essence of his soul; and as if of herself nature will become open to him. Moral action is that great and only experiment in which all riddles, of the most manifold appearances, explain themselves." Wordsworth acted throughout on this principle. No poet was ever less of a dreamer. Volition and self-government are everywhere apparent in his life. He was almost penurious in husbanding his emotions. He shunned and repressed all wasteful excitement, and this, as has been truly said, was one of his most remarkable distinctions among poets, who in spiritual things are often prodigals and spend-thrifts. The contrast with Shelley is here very complete. Wordsworth's own account of the self-culture, or rather self-discipline, which he considered necessary for the development of character, is most characteristic and valuable.

After speaking of the sympathetic melancholy which is roused in a boy's mind as he watches the fitful dying glow of a candle-wick whose flame he has extinguished, he goes on : " Let us accompany the same boy to the period between youth and manhood, when a solicitude may be awakened to the moral life of himself. Are there any powers by which he could call to mind the same image, and hang over it with an equal interest as a visible type of his own perishing spirit? Oh, surely, if the being of the individual be under his own care; if it be his first care; if duty begin from the point of accountableness to our conscience, and, through that, to God and human nature; if, without such primary sense of duty, all secondary care of teacher, of friend or parent, must be baseless and fruitless; if, lastly, the motions of the soul transcend in worth those of the animal functions, nay, give to them their sole value—then truly there are such powers; and the image of the dying taper may be recalled . . . with a melancholy in the soul, *a sinking inward into ourselves from thought to thought, a steady remonstrance, and a high resolve.* Let, then, the youth go back, as occasion will permit, to nature and to solitude. . . . A world of fresh sensations will gradually open upon him, as, instead of being propelled restlessly towards others in admiration, or too hasty love, he makes it his prime business to understand himself." If any of my hearers have been doubting whether I ought to have claimed Wordsworth as a mystic, this description of his own mental methods may perhaps convince them that I was right.

Wordsworth was no dreamer, but an ascetic of an unfamiliar type. His life was one of tense mental discipline, involving continual self-denial, not only by imposing self-chosen limitations in many directions, but in forgoing voluntarily the recognition which a little concession to popular taste would have secured for him before his old age. He knew that he should not be understood : what else could happen "when I think of the pure, absolute, honest ignorance in which worldlings of every rank and situation must be enveloped, with respect to the thoughts, feelings, and

images on which the life of my poems
depends. The things that I have taken,
whether from within or without, what have
they to do with routs, dinners, morning calls?
What have they to do with endless talking
about things that nobody cares anything for,
except as far as their own vanity is concerned,
and with persons they care nothing for, but
as their vanity or selfishness are concerned?
What have they to do (to say all at once)
with a life without love? It is an awful truth
that there neither is nor can be any genuine
enjoyment of poetry among nineteen out of
twenty of these persons who live, or wish to
live, in the broad light of the world—among
those who either are, or are striving to make
themselves, people of consideration in society.
This is a truth and an awful one, because to
be incapable of a feeling of poetry, in my
sense of the word, is to be without love of
human nature and reverence for God." There
are not many instances on record of such a
calm and confident setting aside of the world's
standards, such an unshrinking conviction,
displayed not in word only but in practice,

that a man's life consisteth not in the super-abundance of the things that he possesseth, and that it is "a very small thing" to be judged by man's judgment.

In order to live the life that he had chosen under the most favourable conditions, Words-worth chose a home in that lovely district which has ever since been associated with his name. Of that district it has been truly said that "there is no corner without a meaning and a charm. All agencies have conspired for loveliness, and ruin itself has been benign." It is, moreover, a district which has proved itself favourable to human character. The Cumbrian peasants are not isolated from each other by almost impassable barriers, like the inhabitants of some Swiss valleys. "They have given an example of substantial comfort strenuously won ; of home affections intensified by independent strength ; of isolation without ignorance, and of a shrewd simplicity ; of an hereditary virtue which needs no support from fanaticism, and to which honour is more than law." [1]

---

[1] Myers, *Wordsworth.*

It is a real spiritual privilege to live in such a country. Many people have echoed the words of the Psalmist : " I will lift up mine eyes unto the hills, from whence cometh my help." As repentance, forgiveness, and purification are brought home to us by watching the sea—the great waters never resting from their "priest-like task "[1]—so the larger life of enlightenment, aspiration, and worship becomes ours for a time, when we stand upon a mountain-top, and cast our eyes around and below us. Our Lord Himself was evidently affected by mountain scenery. He loved mountains : the Gospels would be much poorer if the mountain scenes were cut out.[2] And many saintly characters, whose work has been assigned them among the busy haunts of men, have found their best refreshment, for soul as well as body, among the Alps or other mountainous districts. They have found, in the awful grandeur and sublime desolation of snow - peak and precipice, a

---

[1] Compare, too, Euripides' line—

Θάλασσα κλύζει πάντα τάνθρώπων κακά.

[2] This thought is drawn out by W. M. Ramsay, *The Education of Christ.*

bracing tonic after the distracting and unrest-
ful life of the town. The English mountains
are picturesque rather than grand ; but Wordsworth maintained that nothing is lost by the
small size of the Cumberland hills. Three
thousand feet, he thought, is enough to
produce the effect of magnificence. To live
in a place has a different effect upon the mind
from that which is produced by taking a holiday
there. Long familiarity, in Wordsworth's
case, only made his love more discriminating
and his admiration more fervent. Still, a
price has to be paid for living alone with
Nature for many hours every day. Wordsworth's conception of human character was
exceedingly simple. His human material was
a small number of unworldly friends, belonging
to his own class, and a very good type of
peasant. He saw very little of the deeper
and more complex struggles or tragedies of
human life. And, for better or worse, his
interest in humanity was very *impersonal.*
His dreamy little romance about the Highland
girl, whose traits, as he naïvely confesses, he
afterwards transferred to his wife, is an

illustration of this. The processes of his mind
are laid bare in a little poem of uncertain
date, published towards the end of his life :

> "Yes ! thou art fair, yet be not moved
> To scorn the declaration
> That sometimes I in thee have loved
> My fancy's own creation.
>
> .   .   .   .   .
>
> "Be pleased that nature made thee fit
> To feed my heart's devotion,
> By laws to which all forms submit
> In sky, earth, air, and ocean."

Taught too early, as he admits himself, to
feel the self-sufficing power of solitude, he
found little in his manner of life to remedy
a certain hardness and rigidity of mind which
were natural to him.

> "There was a hardness in his cheek,
> There was a hardness in his eye,
> As if the man had fixed his face,
> In many a solitary place,
> Against the wind and open sky."

There is some excuse for Hazlitt's remark
that "had there been no other being in the
universe, Mr Wordsworth's poetry would have
been just what it is." "The note of the
cuckoo sounds in his ear like the voice of

other years; the daisy spreads its leaves in the rays of boyish delight that stream from his thoughtful eyes; the rainbow lifts its proud arch in heaven but to mark his progress from infancy to manhood; an old thorn is buried, bowed down under the mass of associations he has wound about it; and to him, as he himself beautifully says,

> " The meanest flower that blows can give
> Thoughts that do often lie too deep for tears."

This somewhat malicious criticism perhaps only fails to hit the mark because Dorothy Wordsworth was by her brother's side when he wrote much of his best poetry. He owns his debt to her in no stinted language, and his obligation seems to have been just what he says that it was. Within the family circle, at any rate, his affections were warm and steadfast. In this he differs from many contemplative mystics, who have been positively afraid of human affection. " Desire to be familiar only with God and the angels, and fly the acquaintance of men," says Thomas à Kempis. " I was afraid of all company," says George Fox, " for I saw perfectly where

they were, through the love of God which
let me see myself." Wordsworth was afraid
of passionate love, which is a wasteful emotion,
but he desired, a little too self-consciously, to
make the most of quiet affection. But enough
has been said to show that it is not in the
revelation of human character that we shall
find Wordsworth's peculiar message. It is
easier, says a French proverb, to know man
in general than a man in particular; and
Wordsworth seldom particularised men.

But what a message he has left us! In
the sphere of practical ethics our generation
might learn from him what it needs more
than anything else. It is the lesson which
has been taught in the prose of Ruskin not
less eloquently than in the poetry of Wordsworth. "True-heartedness and graciousness,
and undisturbed trust and requited love, and
the sight of the peace of others and the
ministry of their pain; these, and the blue
sky above you, and the sweet waters and
flowers of the earth beneath, and mysteries
and presences innumerable of living beings—
these may yet be here your riches, untorment-

ing and divine, serviceable for the life that now is, nor, it may be, without promise of that which is to come." "We need examples of people who, leaving heaven to decide whether they are to rise in the world, decide for themselves that they will be happy in it, and have resolved to seek, not greater wealth but simpler pleasure, not higher fortune but deeper felicity, making the first of possessions self-possession, and honouring themselves in the harmless pride and calm pursuits of peace." This rational valuation of external goods, which we call Greek because for very shame we cannot call it Christian while *we* are Christians, is combined with a horror of lawless force which is equally Greek. The anti-Napoleonic sonnets supply many examples of this feeling. The insane wickedness of such a career was palpably evident to one who had discovered that all the best gifts of God are lavishly bestowed on all who will take them :

> " The primal duties shine aloft like stars ;
> The charities that soothe and heal and bless
> Are scattered at the feet of men like flowers."

If during the period of our youth, when permanent associations are formed, we have been happy enough to delight in such things, connecting them with the sublime and beautiful in nature, the sight of them afterwards will recall pure and noble sentiments.[1] This is Wordsworth's theory of the religious use of nature, and it is confirmed by experience.

One other application of his principle of spiritual frugality must be mentioned. Most poets have indulged moods of plaintive melancholy ; some have railed at the injustice of things. Wordsworth teaches us how we may transmute and turn to account nearly all our troubles. The Happy Warrior has learned to

> " Exercise a power
> Which is our human nature's highest dower ;
> Controls them and subdues; transmutes, bereaves
> Of their bad influence, and their good receives."

It is a noble doctrine, and, once more, it works. We do take down our Wordsworth, sometimes, when the world goes hardly with us.

But we have not yet justified our inclusion

---

[1] L. Stephen, *Hours in a Library*, vol. ii.

of Wordsworth among the mystics. To do this, we must show that he derived from the contemplation of natural objects a vision of the Divine behind phenomena, of the invisible reality which is hidden behind the world of appearance. There is no lack of evidence that this experience was enjoyed by him frequently. Even in early youth, he tells us:

> " Other pleasures have been mine, and joys
> Of subtler origin ; how I have felt,
> Not seldom even in that tempestuous time,
> Those hallowed and pure motions of the sense,
> Which seem, in their simplicity, to own
> An intellectual charm ; that calm delight
> Which, if I err not, surely must belong
> To those first-born affinities that fit
> Our new existence to existing things,
> And in our dawn of being constitute
> The bond of union between life and joy."

" Those first-born affinities "—this is just what the mystic longs to seize.

> "What if earth
> Be but the shadow of heaven, and things therein
> Each to other like, more than on earth is thought?"

But often Wordsworth experienced that blank trance which, be its explanation what

it may, is a real thing to mystics of all times.
He speaks of occasions,

> "When the light of sense
> Goes out, but with a flash that has revealed
> The invisible world."

Or again—

> "Oft in such moments such a holy calm
> Would overspread my soul, that bodily eyes
> Were utterly forgotten, and what I saw
> Appeared like something in myself, a dream,
> A prospect in my mind."

These sacred moments reveal the underlying
unity in things, and make us contemptuous of

> "That false secondary power
> By which we multiply distinctions, then
> Deem that our puny boundaries are things
> That we perceive, and not that we have made."

The psychology of mysticism is briefly comprehended in some lines from the same poem,
The Prelude :

> "For feeling has to him imparted power
> That through the growing faculties of sense
> Doth like an agent of the one great Mind
> Create, creator and receiver both,
> Working but in alliance with the works
> Which it beholds."

Quite in the Neoplatonic vein, dear to Shelley,
is his mention of

> "Incumbencies more awful, visitings
> Of the Upholder of the tranquil soul,
> That tolerates the indignities of time,
> And, from the centre of Eternity
> All finite motions overruling, lives
> In glory immutable."

The poet, however, is careful to tell us that his
mode of enjoying nature changed as he grew
older. This calm and scrupulous care in
registering his own emotions, which some
have called egoistical, has a real scientific
value, and adds greatly to his usefulness as
an ethical guide. There was a time when
nature was all in all to him, when

> "The tall rock,
> The mountain, and the deep and gloomy wood,
> Their colours and their forms, were then to me
> An appetite ; a feeling and a love,
> That had no need of a remoter charm
> By thought supplied, nor any interest
> Unborrowed from the eye."

Then, in full manhood, a less ecstatic but
deeper emotion was his. "The still, sad
music of humanity," mingled with the rustling

of the leaves and the roaring of the torrent;
and sometimes

> " I have felt
> A presence that disturbs me with the joy
> Of elevated thoughts; a sense sublime
> Of something far more deeply interfused,
> Whose dwelling is the light of setting suns,
> And the round ocean and the living air,
> And the blue sky, and in the mind of man;
> A motion and a spirit that impels
> All thinking things, all objects of all thought,
> And rolls through all things."

The time came when he acknowledged, with
equal candour, that the vision had left him—
the light

> " Full early lost, and fruitlessly deplored;
> Which at the moment on my waking sight
> Appears to shine, by miracle restored!
> My soul, though yet confined to earth,
> Rejoices in a second birth;
> —'Tis past, the visionary splendour fades;
> And night approaches with her shades."

In truth, the poems which have in them the
magic of immediate inspiration were nearly
all written in twenty years of the poet's life
—between 1798 and 1818.

The notion that nature is animated throughout, which, under the name of Pan-psychism,

is an element in some of the best modern philosophy, is clearly recognised by Wordsworth.

"With bliss ineffable
I felt the sentiment of Being spread
O'er all that moves and all that seemeth still."

He "gave a moral life" to every natural form, even the loose stones that cover the highway : "the grea. mass lay bedded in a quickening soul." It follows that some kind of duty and consideration may be due from us even to trees and plants, as he hints in the fine poem called *Nutting*.

A few words must be said about the famous Ode upon the *Intimations of Immortality*. Some critics have said that the idea of this wonderful poem is borrowed from Henry Vaughan, the "Silurist"; but Vaughan gives only a hint of the doctrine which Wordsworth elaborates, and the credit of originality must not be withheld from the later poet. The theme of the poem—the dignity and sacredness of our childish instincts, is not bound up with any theory of pre-existence or Platonic *anamnesis*—theories which Wordsworth himself certainly did not hold in any definite form. The subject is one of surpassing interest, because modern psychological science ascribes great importance to the racial consciousness as a factor in individual character, and is quite at one with Wordsworth in treating the child-nature with the utmost respect. Wordsworth, it may be conjectured, would not have been a disciple of Darwin; he would have been "on the side of the angels"; but on the main point they were agreed. Man has instincts which do not arise from his own experience in his present life. And, the poet would add, those instincts, which appear to have a longer history than our individual lifetime, have a peculiar sacredness, and should be cherished with especial reverence. Further than this we shall perhaps be unwilling to follow him. There seems to be no reason why, as we get older, we should recede further from knowledge of Divine truth. The natural exhilaration of spirits, which in the child is stimulated by fresh air and fine weather, is in most cases hardly worthy to be called a splendid vision; and the light of common day

into which it is said to fade is after all the
light of mature intelligence and ripe experience.
The glories of poetic imagination, which, as we
have seen, only shone with their full effulgence
for about twenty years of Wordsworth's life,
are an abnormal gift, and we need not suppose
that ordinary experience follows the same laws.

What, then, are the lessons which the
contemplation of nature has to teach us?
"Unworldliness" would not be a bad answer.
Principal Shairp says very truly: "You will
never find the mere man of the world, who
takes his tone from society, really care for
Wordsworth's poetry." Wordsworth schooled
himself not to "feel contempt for any living
thing"; but there was one pardonable
exception: he had the heartiest contempt for
the mere man and woman of fashion; "convinced at heart, how vain a correspondence
with the talking world proves to the most."
Converse with nature opens our eyes; we
cannot any longer mistake artificialities for
real substance. We may call Wordsworth's
attitude truly democratic or truly aristocratic,
whichever we please; the two ideals are not

far apart, though their corruptions are poles
asunder. The extremely simple diction which
he cultivated is both aristocratic and democratic. What Bagehot called "a dressy
literature, an exaggerated literature — the
curse of our times," is the product of an
age which is neither aristocratic nor democratic, but vulgar. Wordsworth bids us

> "bend in reverence
> To Nature, and the power of human minds,
> To men as they are men within themselves."

"Obeisance paid where it is due"—such is
the proud and humble attitude of Nature's
priest when in the presence of his fellow-
men. And in the presence of God, he will
not, like some scientific investigators, stop
short at the revelation of law and order
which is impressed upon the visible world
(the recognition of τάξις and πέρας which Plotinus
rightly insisted on as a valuable though early
lesson in the spiritual course), but will understand the true and eternal significance of the
Greek Logos-theology which is just now so
unhappily disparaged by Continental thinkers.
I will conclude this Lecture by a quotation from

Athanasius, which is not far from Wordsworth's own theological attitude. "The all-
powerful, all-perfect, and all-holy Word of the
Father, descending upon all things, and everywhere extending His own energy, and bringing
to light all things, whether visible or invisible,
knits and welds them into His own being,
leaving nothing destitute of His operation.
And a certain marvellous and Divine harmony
is thus veritably brought to pass by Him."

LECTURE VI

THE MYSTICISM OF ROBERT BROWNING

ROBERT BROWNING was once asked by a friend whether he cared much for nature. " Yes, a great deal," he replied : " but for human beings a great deal more." [1] No reader of his poems can fail to see that this is true, and also that the poet was right in saying " human beings," not " humanity." Browning loved and studied, not mankind, but men. He is, therefore, complementary to Wordsworth ; he might be called the Wordsworth of human nature. We may rightly call him a mystic, in virtue of his profound belief in a perfect spiritual world, in which all broken fragments are made whole, all riddles solved, and all legitimate hopes

---

[1] So in the Dedication to *Sordello* he says : " Little else [besides the development of a soul] is worth study : I, at least, always thought so."

satisfied. A strong hunger for eternity and perfection, combined with close and reverent handling of the facts of life; a tenacious grip of the concrete finite example, with a determination to make it illustrate, and be illustrated by, its ideal and spiritual principle; —this is the method of the true mystic, and in all that concerns human character it is the method of Browning. I shall therefore not be afraid of classing him with a type of humanity which in some ways seems so opposite to his own. This breezy optimist, who faced the difficulties of life by charging them as a bull goes at a fence, who had so firm a hold of the actual and concrete, was certainly not a *mere* mystic. But that there was a mystical element in his genius and his teaching, and that this element constitutes a very valuable part of his message, is a proposition which I think easy to establish, and which I hope will be acknowledged to be true by those who follow me in what I am about to say.

My present task is more difficult than that which I attempted in my last Lecture, because

while Wordsworth's poetry is totally destitute of
the dramatic element, Browning is particularly
anxious that the dramatic character of his
poems should not be forgotten. He will not
believe that Shakespeare ever "unlocked his
heart" for his readers, and does not wish his
own readers to assume that they have the
key to the heart of Robert Browning.

> "Which of you did I enable
> Once to slip inside my breast,
> There to catalogue and label
> What I like least, what love best?"

Only in a few poems, such as *One Word
More, Prospice,* and perhaps *Christmas Eve
and Easter Day,* can we be sure that he is
speaking in his own person.

When Browning began to write, natural
science was being preached as a complete
gospel, with a confidence which has now
abated considerably. Few had then suspected
that science could be other than materialistic,
or could make terms with metaphysics. The
spiritualistic monism which is now embraced
by many physicists would have been scouted

2 D

by their predecessors. Science at that time threatened to become what Lucretius describes religion as being—a horrible spectre standing in the path of humanity, forbidding hope and faith, casting its icy hand even upon love, and offering no comfort save in unconditional submission to a mechanical order, in which neither purpose nor goodness could be traced. Idealism was treated as a deliberate sojourn in dreamland; *men* were absorbed in "mankind." Until about the last twenty years of his life Browning was swimming against the stream almost as much as Wordsworth was in the great period of his productiveness. He is never tired of insisting on the relativity and inadequacy of scientific knowledge, and on the necessary falsehood of a philosophy of life which ignores the affections or denies the validity of their intuitions. He is the sworn foe of intellectualism, which he pursues with such animosity that occasionally he seems to have declared war even against the intellect. This polemical attitude must be judged with reference to the dominant tendencies of thought at the time when he began to write.

In his old age it cannot be denied that he pushed his protest too far, and at a time when the opposite error had ceased to be aggressive.

Browning is the poet of *personality*. Amiel considered that "to depersonalise man is the great tendency of our age." This tendency found an unrelenting antagonist in Browning. Any attempt to belittle man, or rather men, by comparison with natural forces aroused his ire.

> " 'O littleness of man !' deplores the bard ;
> And then, for fear the powers should punish him,
> 'O grandeur of the visible universe,
> Our human littleness contrasts withal ;
> O sun, O moon, ye mountains, and thou sea,
> Thou emblem of immensity, thou this
> That and the other—what impertinence
> In man to eat and drink and walk about,
> And have his little notions of his own,
> The while some wave sheds foam upon the shore.' "

We recognise here a revolt against the assumption that the value of things depends on their bulk, or universality. Kant, as every one knows, bowed his head in reverence before two things — the star-sown deep of

space, and the moral consciousness of mankind. Natural science seemed to threaten to
leave us only the former object of worship.
Browning claimed a truer greatness for the
latter, not as a general idea, but in its
individual manifestations.

And yet he was no enemy to the new
discoveries. The *organic* idea was grasped
and utilised by him, as by few others of his
generation. We are not to look for complete-
ness either in the present divorced from the
past and future, or in the individual life
divorced from that of other individuals. "The
race of man . . . receives life in parts to live
in a whole." And the "whole," in which we
are to strive "resolutely" (as Goethe also
tells us) to live, is a whole which gathers
into a unity all the partial and faulty manifestations of reality which occur as successive events
in the time-process, and all the fragmentary
souls which are born separate only that they
may feel the need of mingling, and by mingling
may attain their true rights and full development as persons. The doctrine of pre-
existence, in some form not easy to grasp,

is a more serious part of Browning's teaching
than of Wordsworth's.

> " Doubt you if, in some such moment,
>   As she fixed me, she felt clearly,
> Ages past the soul existed,
>   Here an age 'tis resting merely
>
> " And hence fleets again for ages,
>   While the true end, sole and single,
> It stops here for is this love-way,
>   With some other soul to mingle ? "

Humanity is incarnated in each man, but
each man is only realised so far as he
passes out of himself into the wider life of
humanity.

Carlyle was contemptuous of the charge of
pantheism, which was brought against him as
against others who have grasped the organic
view of human life and history. He thought
it, at any rate, a better creed than what he
called the " pot-theism " of the Calvinist. But
pantheism has many developments. We
cannot even say whether a thorough-going
pessimism or a thorough-going optimism is
the more legitimate outcome of its principles.
It is interesting to contrast the gloomy
outlook of Carlyle with the facile cheerfulness

of Emerson, when we consider how closely akin they are in their view of reality. Emerson's creed is true pantheism—the old Oriental philosophy which sees the divine equally in everything; while Carlyle has very little belief in any divine immanence except as the voice of conscience uttering commands and threats. Such a view of the relation between God and man was sure to carry with it a stern and dark philosophy of life. Browning agrees with neither of them. His message is his own. He stakes everything on the non-existence of absolute evil. He holds that there is a natural tendency towards good in all men—a victorious striving upward which is our natural and healthy activity, and which can never be wholly destroyed. We are reminded of the supposed faculty of *synteresis*, about which scholastic mystics like the Victorines and Bonaventura discourse learnedly — the divinely implanted centre of the soul which can never consent to sin. Browning sees a silvery lining to the blackest cloud. Though at times all seems dark—

> " All the same
> Of absolute and irretrievable
> And all-subduing black—black's soul of black
> Beyond white's power to disintensify—
> Of that I saw no trace."

This kindly and hopeful view of human nature is always given by Browning as the result of his observation. His high spirits are the reflection in feeling of an experience of men which has led him to the conclusion that there is none that doeth ill—pure unmixed evil—no, not one. Hence his love for dissecting a knave's soul, and showing that the scoundrel is a human being, with whose point of view it is even possible to feel some sympathy. The worldly agnostic bishop, the vulgar spiritualist "medium," the painter of Madonnas caught in low haunts, even the bishop who orders his tomb in St Praxed's Church, are not odious; there is something not wholly vile in each of them. He will not accept the rough-and-ready division of human beings into sheep and goats. There is much in every character which the world's coarse thumb and finger fails to plumb. It is not for us to stick a label on to a man,

and say that such is his character. Original
sin is a defect imposed on us by God for
our final good; it is not a total corruption
of our nature. A human being cannot be
wholly bad. "Even badness," says Plotinus,
"is still human, and is mixed with something
contrary to itself." If a man or a thing were
wholly bad, it would fall to pieces and cease
in mere nothingness. Giuseppe Caponsacchi
sees Guido gliding down from depth to depth
of infamy,

> "Till at the doleful end,
> At the horizontal line, creation's verge,
> From what just is to absolute nothingness—
> Whom is it, straining onward still, he meets?"

By a merciful decree, God has made dissolution
the penalty of moral evil, so that what is
incurable soon passes into annihilation.

Browning is a firm believer in teleology. A
purpose runs through all that happens in the
world. But the purpose is the redemption of
individual lives. "In the seeing soul all
worth lies." "Progress," in the sense in
which the word was constantly used by the
confident scientists of Browning's generation,

appealed to him very little. He regarded
life as the battle-ground on which the struggle
for an autonomous moral personality is to be
fought out. The combatants are free will
and circumstance; the life succeeds—the man
gains what he lived for—in proportion as
free will is able to assert its supremacy over
circumstance. Difficulty, pain, and even sin,
may be factors in the victory of will —
needful elements in its emancipation from the
tyranny of circumstance. But whereas man
"partly is, and wholly hopes to be" (his
condition of *becoming* being, indeed, his great
characteristic, distinguishing him from higher
and lower existences, which simply *are*), no
classification of him by hard and fast names
can be true. It is his privilege to be
imperfect; his shortcomings are, in a sense,
the measure of his potential greatness. "Our
present life," says Bishop Westcott,[1] "is to be
taken in its entirety. The discipline of man
is to be fulfilled, the progress of man is to be
secured, under the conditions of our complex

---

[1] "Browning's View of Life," in *Religious Thought of the
West*, p. 257.

earthly being. These lets and limitations are
not to be disparaged or overborne, but accepted
and used in due order. No attempt must be
made either to retain that which has been,
or to anticipate that which will be. Each
element in human nature is to be allowed its
proper office. Each season brings its own
work and its own means." The lessons of
advancing years are taught in *Rabbi ben
Ezra* :—

> "Grow old along with me!
> The best is yet to be,
> The last of life, for which the first was made:
> Our times are in His hand
> Who saith, 'A whole I planned,
> Youth shows but half;' trust God; see all, nor
> be afraid."

According to Browning, salvation is only
to be won by obedience to the laws of the
universe. In this he agrees with the ethics
of naturalism. But he has very distinct views
as to what the laws of the universe are.
Most thinkers construct their world out of
some one constitutive principle, which serves
as an explanation of the general scheme.
With Hegel it is reason; with Schopenhauer

it is will; some writers have regarded
mechanical uniformity as the law, the end,
and aim of all Nature's activities. Browning's
constitutive principle is *Love*. Love and
reciprocity of life are the condition and
necessary expression of human perfection.
The comparative poverty of our language,
which comprehends under one name such
different emotions as sexual love, love of
parents, and love of country, enabled Browning to present his constitutive principle under
various aspects. But it is distinctly sexual
love, not Christian charity—ἔρως, not ἀγάπη—
which he considers to possess the key of
life's real meaning. He is not ashamed of
its connection with and growth out of the
instincts which we share with the lower
animals. Its true nature is not to be sought
in its origin, but in its completed development.
And love, in its perfect state, is a principle of
moral activity, a mode of the expansion of
the self into universal and eternal relations.
No other poet has set himself to show, under
so many different aspects, the immense importance of love in the growth of the soul.

The essence of love is going out of oneself, shifting the centre of our lives outside the merely self-regarding sphere. Therefore sensuality and brutal lust, so far from being the reality of love when its clothes and trappings have been stripped off, are the perversion of love, and even its contradictory. For lust is the extreme of selfishness, which does not hesitate to sacrifice others to itself. True love may begin with a large element of bodily appetite; but it issues in a communion of souls, in which each makes the other see "new depths of the divine."

> "But who could have expected this
> When we two drew together first
> Just for the obvious human bliss,
> To satisfy life's daily thirst
> With a thing men seldom miss?"

Love is the "spark God gave us from His fire of fires." We need fear nothing "while that burns on, though all the rest grow dark." This favourite doctrine and metaphor of mysticism, that of the ψυχῆς κέντρον of Plotinus, the "Funkelein" of Eckhart, is thus connected by our poet with love of the

opposite sex. This would have shocked in-
expressibly many of the earlier Christian
mystics; but Browning has no quarrel with
the flesh, as flesh. To quote Krause, whose
beautiful little book, *The Ideals of Humanity*,
is in many ways an admirable commentary on
Browning's poetry, "spirit and body in man
are equally original, equally living, equally
divine; they claim to be maintained in the
same purity and holiness, and to be equally
loved and developed." " Neither nature nor
reason," says the same writer, "undertakes
to give man form and maintenance as an
individual being. Hence the highest wisdom
and goodness has implanted in every breast
a longing for other human beings, and for
their companionship and love." This desire
for companionship and communion shows itself
in all parts of our nature, and is innocent and
right in all.

Browning is the hierophant of these new
mysteries. He shows us under innumerable
examples how love can guide us into all
truth, and how those who refuse opportunities
of sharing this highest of our privileges are

in danger of losing eternally what they lived for. It is a mystical philosophy, based on a sacramental view of experience. What makes Browning such an original teacher is that none else has believed so whole-heartedly in the advantages of this particular "pathway to reality," or has described so completely the ground which we shall traverse if we follow it.

It is too much to expect that a thinker with so strong a bent in one direction should do justice to views which are antagonistic or even only complementary to his own. We have seen how he speaks with impatience, almost with contempt, of the æsthetic contemplation of nature without reference to human interests. We must now add that he shows an excessive and an increasing distrust of the intellectual faculties as a means of bringing us to God. The error, if it is an error, cannot be easily removed from his philosophy, because it is intimately bound up with his doctrine of imperfection. As long as life and development go on, our scheme of ultimate truth cannot be rounded off. In the speculative thought of finite, growing beings, there must always be a heel of Achilles—a vulnerable point which may prove fatal to the whole. Behind our clearest consciousness there are latent coefficients, and a dark chaos of tendencies and dispositions, out of which our consciousness works itself. It is useless, he thinks, to attempt to construct a system out of such imperfect material. Our intellectual faculties, our æsthetic faculties—in fact, all the contents of our minds, with the exception of our affections—are flawed. Love only is Divine, and a guide whom we may trust implicitly. The constant "tendency to God" which he finds in human nature is bound up with the heart and will, not with the intellect. On this side Browning is an ultra-mystic. He considers that discursive thought plays round about the facts without ever reaching them. Such a theory of knowledge leads logically to complete scepticism, a theory which is almost crudely avowed in a late poem, *A Pillar of Sebzevar.* Knowledge, it appears, always deludes us with false hopes. We crown our brows with it, but each garland is pushed off by another, which proves nowise more constant; to-day's gain is to-morrow's loss; knowledge the golden turns out to be only lacquered ignorance; what seemed ore proves when assayed to be but dross. The prize of knowledge is in the process of acquiring it, in the ever-renewed assurance by defeat that victory may still be reached; but love is victory, the prize itself.

> "Wholly distrust thy knowledge, then, and trust
> As wholly love allied to ignorance!"

And again—

> "So let us say—not, Since we know, we love,
> But rather, Since we love, we know enough."

The reaction against intellectualism could go no further than this. By way of complete contrast, let us recall the ingredients of blessedness according to Spinoza. They are (1) knowledge of the causes of things, (2) control of our passions, (3) sound health. It is true that love, even in Spinoza, comes in at the summit of the ascent. But the *amor intellectualis Dei*, which constitutes the beatific vision for Spinoza, is far enough from the

"love allied to ignorance" which Browning
came to consider the happiest state.

How came a learned poet, whose intellectual
curiosity, assisted by a wonderful memory, has
left its impress on nearly every page of his
writings, to pour scorn on the noblest of his
own endowments, and preach what looks
like mere sentimentalism and emotionalism?
Perhaps the problem of evil has something
to do with it. For to the intellect evil must
be either real or not real. But if it is real,
optimism is destroyed. And if it is not
real, morality is destroyed. Browning will
not surrender a jot of the claims of either
optimism or morality. Therefore, since these
claims, when judged by the intellect, are
manifestly incompatible with each other,
there is no help for it but to assert that
the intellect is essentially self-stultifying.
Hence Browning's intellectual pessimism,
which is simply the price which he is willing
to pay for his moral and emotional optimism.

But this disparagement of intellect is
suicidal. It is impossible to sunder the mind
from the heart so completely as to follow the

one blindly, while "wholly distrusting" the
other. This personification of our faculties,
as rival claimants to our confidence, is really
almost absurd. We cannot love what we do
not know: perhaps we cannot truly know
what we do not love. Knowledge and love
are not two mutually exclusive faculties.
Love is the culminating point in a series of
which knowledge is the last stage but one,
and the condition of reaching the highest.
The fact that we cannot round off our intellectual system of the universe, that our theory
seems always to halt at one point, is, when
rightly considered, not a reason for "wholly
distrusting" reason, but for trusting it. We
know why it *cannot* tell us everything. The
reason is that we are less than that which
we desire to comprehend. Browning's own
doctrine of the value of the time-process,
which leads us through imperfection to our
goal, should teach us not to despise or distrust
imperfect knowledge. This is life eternal,
says the Fourth Gospel, that we should know
God and Jesus Christ. Not "knowledge," a
word which, like "faith," St John studiously

avoids, but the process of knowing, the life of learning, this is eternal life. A faith which is sceptical on the intellectual side, which acquiesces in ignorance, and fills the void with the products of mere emotion, is a house built upon the sand. Browning, to do him justice, is not so far from admitting this, as the quotations made just now would lead us to think. "The heart," it has been well said, "quarrels with reasons, not with reason;" and this is really Browning's position. His homage to love is based on reason. Knowledge and love are two forms of experience; and experience (he would probably have admitted) is the ultimate metaphysical reality. Love is the purest form in which reality is presented to us, since it is not given us in shreds and patches, but in its essence. As the old theologians said, There is no gift, except love, in which the giver gives himself.

An interesting parallel to Browning's teaching about love as the highest law of life is the chapter about love as the reconciling principle of knowledge and volition, in Mr McTaggart's *Studies in Hegelian*

Dialectic. " The concrete and material content of a life of perfected knowledge and volition means one thing only — love." And he continues that, since perfection alone deserves love, love in an imperfect world must be love of the person as he really is—that is, as he will be. Love is unreasonable only because reason is not yet worthy of it. In the perfect life knowledge and volition will be swallowed up in a higher reality, and love will reveal itself as the only thing in the universe. ("Whether there be prophecies, they shall fail; whether there be knowledge, it shall vanish away.") The distinction between knowledge and volition can have no place in the absolute perfection. The true and the good, which seem now so different, can only be harmonised by "emotion." Knowledge and volition both postulate an ideal which they can never reach while they remain knowledge and volition. The element of Not-Self is essential to both, but is incompatible with their perfection. But in the case of love this contradiction is overcome. We regard the person whom we love as we regard ourselves.

The chief difference between the scheme here sketched and Browning's teaching, is that the latter attributes only a subordinate place to the intellect and to "knowledge." And "emotion," in his poetry, seems often not so much to reconcile knowledge and volition, as to override them both.

The other great poet of the Victorian era is at one with Browning in his revolt against intellectualism. In a well-known stanza of *In Memoriam* Tennyson says:

> "A warmth within the soul would melt
> The freezing reason's colder part,
> And like a man in wrath, the heart
> Stood up and answered, I have felt."

This is at any rate a good description of the methods of emotionalism, which gives us heat instead of light, and vehement assertion instead of argument. But the claim of the heart to be heard may be admitted without leaving reason quite out in the cold.

Some may think that Tennyson would have been a better example of mysticism in contemporary poetry than Browning. I cannot agree with this view. Poems like the

Ancient Sage certainly show knowledge and appreciation of mysticism, and his biography shows that he was no stranger to the mystical trance. But Tennyson's ethics are decidedly anti-mystical. The moral of his Arthurian epic really seems to be: "Do not pursue the Holy Grail, but obey your king, and be dutiful and active in practical life." In Tennyson the quest of the Holy Grail has as much to do with wrecking Arthur's great scheme, as Guinevere's unfaithfulness. Browning, we may be sure, would have made the Grail the centre of his story. It would have been *never* attained even by Galahad, but in the search for it the true knights would have done their life's work, and received, in doing it, their reward. In that unattainable ideal would have lain realisation of all attainable nobleness, and success for those who pursued it. This doctrine is very finely expounded in *Colombe's Birthday :*—

> "One great aim, like a guiding-star, above—
> Which tasks strength, wisdom, stateliness, to lift
> His manhood to the height that takes the prize;
> A prize not near—lest overlooking earth

He rashly spring to seize it—nor remote,
So that he rest upon his path content:
But day by day, while shimmering grows shine,
And the faint circlet prophesies the orb,
He sees so much as, just evolving these,
The stateliness, the wisdom, and the strength,
To due completion, will suffice this life,
And lead him at his grandest to the grave."

For Tennyson, the individual is less, and society more. He has (at least in the first half of his poetical career) a real belief in "progress," as preached by the science of his generation. He believed that the ape and tiger were being gradually eliminated. And in this process, knowledge and improved organisation are naturally important factors. The unreasoning passions must be curbed and repressed; undisciplined aspirations must be sternly discouraged. All this is quite foreign to Browning. Progress, for him, is in the individual, not in the race, and obedience to law means very little to him. It is better to trust our deepest and strongest instincts than any conventional code. Earthly life is only a means of ascent to God. While we are climbing spiritually, earthly failures do not matter at all, and even sins do not matter much. Browning's teaching is in danger of antinomianism, as one or two poems—*The Flight of the Duchess* and *The Statue and the Bust*, for example—prove. This is chiefly apparent when he is dealing with the subject of love. In Tennyson's eyes the danger is the gratification of passion in violation of law or conscience. In Browning, the danger is that we may sacrifice an ennobling passion to the world—to considerations of prudence or fear of public opinion. This explains his admiration for the unconventional life of the Bohemian artist. "Under the present conditions of industrial life, the artist is almost the only workman who can without reserve set himself to do his best."[1] Moreover, the artist knows that "richness of emotional life determines the intensity of the vision." Our heritage of glorious passion can not only be squandered —that we all know well enough—but it can also be hoarded till it perishes unused; and

---

[1] Granger, *The Soul of a Christian*, p. 174.

this is perhaps a more complete failure than the other. The spendthrift of his emotions gets something; the miser of them may gain the whole world, but he has lost his own soul. Browning's ethics are thus the very opposite of the meticulous counsels of mediæval Catholicism. To have avoided positive sins is a small matter for congratulation; to have missed opportunities of fulness of life is a great matter for blame. So he dares to say:

> " Let a man contend to the uttermost
> For his life's set prize, be it what it will !
> .   .   .   .
> And the sin I impute to each frustrate ghost
> Is the unlit lamp and the ungirt loin,
> Though the end in sight was a vice, I say."

Low aims, despondency, and cowardice are the cardinal vices for Robert Browning, and next to these, intellectual arrogance. The basis of his religion was the conviction that there is a witness to the presence of God in the spirit of man; a witness which declares itself in gleams and glimpses, "when the spirit's true endowments stand out plainly from its false ones." Even the worldly and

2 G

disingenuous priest, Bishop Blougram, is made
to say :—

> "Just when we're safest, there's a sunset touch,
> A fancy from a flower-bell, some one's death,
> A chorus ending from Euripides,—
> And that's enough for fifty hopes and fears
> As old and new at once as Nature's self,
> To rap and knock and enter in our soul,
> Take hands and dance there, a fantastic ring,
> Round the ancient idol, on his base again,
> The great Perhaps."

But religion is not for him "the great
Perhaps." He holds that assurance and
illumination come to those who follow their
noblest instincts—the instincts of love and
healthy activity—and never doubt or look
back. This confidence, which never flagged
to the last, made him something better than
an optimist—it made him a happy man. He
was thoroughly convinced that the scheme
of things means well, and that all things
must work together for good to those who
love God. And, believing as he did in the
continuity of existence, he felt scorn for
those who fear death. "Death, death," he
said, "it is this harping on death that I

despise so much, In fiction, in poetry, in
art, in literature, the shadow of death, call it
what you will—despair, negation, indifference
—is upon us. But what fools who talk thus!
Why, *amico mio*, you know as well as I that
death is life, just as our daily momentarily
dying body is none the less alive, and ever
recruiting new forces of existence. Without
death, which is our church-yardy, crape-like
word for change, for growth, there could be
no prolongation of that which we call life.
Never say of me that I am dead." The
same brave spirit appears in the poem
Prospice, which perhaps gives us as clear a
glimpse of the poet's inmost soul as any
other ; and in the *Epilogue*, which is printed
as his word of farewell. Death means very
little to a Christian ; and to dwell in thought
upon it, to gloat over it, to grow sentimental
or maudlin about it, to harp upon it, in
Browning's own phrase, is mere faithlessness
or vulgarity. "There is no subject," says
Spinoza, who for once may be quoted on
the same side as Browning, "on which the
wise man will think so seldom as on death."

There is one other point in Browning's mysticism which calls for a few words before I conclude. No poet before him had realised so fully the profound significance of the apparently trivial. Other poets have chosen themes for tragedy from the misfortunes of princes, or the clash of supernatural and Titanic forces. Browning can find a theme as elevating in a common police-case. Wordsworth had often found thoughts too deep for tears in the meanest flower. Tennyson had reflected that a tiny plant growing on a wall contains implicitly the secret of what God and man is. But to find the universal significance of human meanness is a rarer gift. The murdering villain of the *Ring and the Book*, a licentious monk, a detected swindler, an agnostic priest—who before Browning had thought of a sympathetic study of such characters? There is something at once profoundly Christian and thoroughly scientific in his method. It belongs to his own generation, and still more perhaps to the younger generation whom he lived to teach; but it was also, if we may say it reverently, the method of Jesus Christ, who despaired of nobody except a Pharisee, and counted nothing common or unclean. And if mysticism is correctly defined as the habit of mind which discerns the spiritual in common things, Browning may certainly be claimed as one of the band, in virtue of his manner of regarding ordinary human nature.

I think that I have now justified the statement which I made in my opening lecture, that the mystical type of religious thought has been well represented in our literature. I have chosen examples as widely different from each other as could be found anywhere. No two lives could be more unlike than that of a mediæval anchoress, and that of the nineteenth century poet who lived much in society and enjoyed it. But the votaries of the inner light have something in common which goes deeper than the accidents of social position and outward habits. They agree in looking within themselves for their authority in matters of belief. It is this which makes the study of mysticism and mystical writers so attractive to many in our generation. Thousands are craving for a basis of belief which shall rest, not on tradition or authority or historical evidence, but on the ascertainable facts of human experience. And the mystics, it has been truly said, are the only through-going empiricists. They guide us to the perennial "fresh springs" of religion, and present it to us as a living and active force, as palpable and undeniable as the so-called "forces of nature," though less easy to explain and control. Whether psychology will ever reduce the phenomena of mysticism to rule, it is impossible to say. If it does, the validity of the testimony will be in no way impaired. It is to the study of religious experience that faith must look for the reinforcement which it needs against its many enemies. The religions of authority are tottering to their fall; but the religion of the Spirit is still near the beginning of that triumphant course which Christ foretold for it on the last evening of His life: "When He, the Spirit of Truth, is come, He will guide you into all truth. . . . He will glorify Me; for He will take of Mine, and will show it unto you." It is to the guidance of that Spirit, which, through manifold diversities of operations, divides to every man severally as He will, yet works in all harmoniously towards one end, that the Church of the twentieth century must commit itself for guidance; not spurning the counsels of those who hold no ministerial commission to preach or teach, but welcoming from every quarter the testimony of those whose hearts God has touched.